CASUAL, ELEGANT KNITS

CLASSY DESIGNS FOR WOMEN AND MEN

FAINA GOBERSTEIN AND DAWN LEESEMAN

Martingale®
& COMPANY

ACKNOWLEDGMENTS

Our special thanks to our families for their support, encouragement, and patience during the time we were working on this book.

A big thank you to Joanne Wilson, the owner of HeartStrings Yarn Studio in Chico, California, for her friendship, for believing in us, and for encouraging us to write this book. We appreciate her listening to our problems and providing the creative atmosphere in her shop.

Many thanks go to:

Danny Leeseman, for his endless support and for being available any time we needed his help.

Simon Goberstein, for his support, patience, and all the help with initial modeling, proofreading, and for being there for us with great feedback.

We also would like to thank our test knitters: Roni Scofield, Rachel Iufer, Pam Morrell, Debbie Sbragia, and Laura Lackey.

A very special thank you to our initial model, Kelley Smith.

Our deep appreciation to Ron and Yvonne Schwager of Schwager Studios for their time and beautiful work on our portraits.

We are grateful to the following yarn companies: Berroco, Cascade Yarns, Crystal Palace Yarns, Fiesta Yarns, Karabella Yarns, Louet, NY Yarns, and Rowan Yarns for their generosity and support of this book.

Our very special thank-you to our wonderful technical editor, Ursula Reikes.

We also would like to thank everyone at Martingale & Company who worked so hard on the production of this book, especially Tami Aderrab, Mary Green, Tina Cook, Kathleen Cubley, Karen Soltys, Stan Green, and Brent Kane.

Casual, Elegant Knits: Classy Designs for Women and Men

© 2008 by Faina Goberstein and Dawn Leeseman

Martingale®
& COMPANY

Martingale & Company®
20205 144th Ave. NE
Woodinville, WA 98072-8478 USA
www.martingale-pub.com

Printed in China
13 12 11 10 09 08   8 7 6 5 4 3 2 1

Library of Congress Cataloging-in-Publication Data
Library of Congress Control Number: 2008012225

ISBN: 978-1-56477-840-6

CREDITS

President & CEO — Tom Wierzbicki

Publisher — Jane Hamada

Editorial Director — Mary V. Green

Managing Editor — Tina Cook

Developmental Editor — Karen Costello Soltys

Technical Editor — Ursula Reikes

Copy Editor — Kathleen Cubley

Design Director — Stan Green

Production Manager — Regina Girard

Illustrators — Robin Strobel & Adrienne Smitke

Cover & Text Designer — Shelly Garrison

Photographer — Brent Kane

MISSION STATEMENT

Dedicated to providing
quality products and service
to inspire creativity.

CONTENTS

Casual, Elegant Knits offers an exciting collection of knitwear for men and women. Here you will find something unique and useful no matter what your knitting skills are, basic or advanced. We have created an attractive and balanced assortment of classic and sophisticated designs, most of which are not technically complicated.

In our carefully chosen ensembles, "City Life" and "Elegant Afternoon," you will find well-coordinated outfits grouped together with style and color in mind for that put-together look. The designs in these ensembles reflect the mood in each scene. Our third collection, "Gotta Have It," consists of irresistible accessories that you've just, well, gotta have!

When you peruse through our collections, you will appreciate each design individually. Any of these pieces can become a favorite addition to your wardrobe. We have paid equal attention to both men's and women's couture. Our inspiration for these designs came from knowing that busy schedules allow little time for a change of clothes when you need to go from work to social events or an evening on the town. That's why we designed knitwear that is comfortable and stylish enough to look equally great at work and elsewhere.

For our first ensemble, "City Life," we chose three bold colors: red, gray, and black. This combination makes a fashion statement by itself. There are eleven items in this ensemble, including a skirt, sweaters, hats, bags, and scarves for him or her. These designs are fun to knit and a pleasure to wear.

Our second ensemble, "Elegant Afternoon," features a wider range of colors, which is more suitable for time spent away from work. This collection offers seven elegant designs: a skirt, a top, a shawl, and a bag for her; a polo shirt, a bag, and a hat for him. You will enjoy working with the variety of luxurious yarns that we have selected for these garments.

The final collection, "Gotta Have It," offers six fun-to-make accessories: two hats, two scarves, and two pairs of fingerless gloves that any knitter will be tempted to make. Each of these small projects is a perfect gift item, although you surely won't be able to resist knitting several items for yourself.

There is something for everyone in our book; the majority of patterns are written for several sizes and many of the designs are unisex. By suggesting how to put the outfits together, we have tried to free you from the guesswork of how to combine different designs. At the same time, as a fashion-conscious knitter, you might want to experiment with your own color palette, and we definitely encourage you to do that.

We have combined the best of our qualities as knitters and designers and have blended our European and American backgrounds to come up with unique pieces. We have always admired fashionable knitwear for both genders, complemented by unique accessories. Individually, we have created numerous garments, experimented with color and texture, and written many patterns that have been in high demand. We have also taught and inspired many students who in turn inspired us in our work. Many people have encouraged us to share our passion and knowledge with a bigger community of fellow knitters. As a result, we have decided to go on the journey of jointly writing this book, which has turned out to be an exciting and rewarding project for both of us.

We invite you to share with us our passion for the beautiful craft of knitting.

Faina and *Dawn*

We have put a lot of effort into making our instructions clear and easy to follow. We believe that an enthusiastic knitter would want to do every project, no matter how small or easy, with care and correct finishing techniques, so that when completed, it will have a truly professional look. For this reason, we would like to bring your attention to a few important points for successful knitting.

GAUGE SWATCH

It is essential that you start working on a pattern by making a gauge swatch using the yarn you choose for the project, needles, and stitch pattern recommended in the instructions. Take your time making the swatch. We suggest that you make a 6" x 6" swatch. Carefully measure in the middle of the swatch how many stitches are in 4". The reason for this is that the gauge is more accurate in the middle than at the edges.

If the number of stitches is higher than recommended, knit another swatch using a larger needle. If the number of stitches is less than recommended, knit another swatch using a smaller needle. Your goal should be to obtain the gauge given in the pattern (the needle size doesn't matter). Block your swatch and recheck your gauge to make sure that you have the required number of stitches. Doing so ensures that your garment will fit you perfectly.

READING THE PATTERN

Before you start knitting, read the pattern and make sure you understand the abbreviations. Consult the list of abbreviations on page 89 if you are unfamiliar with any of them. Please refer to diagrams and schematics, if the pattern provides them. They contain additional information that you will find helpful.

READING THE CHART

Some projects include charts for the stitch patterns. We consider a chart to be a visual aid for a knitter. Each chart is clearly marked with row numbers and right side (RS) and wrong side (WS) rows. The symbols used in the charts are uniform throughout the book. Next to the chart, you will find a key that correlates to the symbols and abbreviations in the pattern. The set up of the chart imitates your knitting direction from the bottom up. If there is a pattern repeat, it is indicated with a bold line around it, as in the Ribbing with a Twist chart (flat) on page 12. Stitches before and after that area are worked once. Take time to learn how to use the charts and you will love them.

TECHNIQUES

We are very particular about certain techniques used in this book. Refer to "Techniques" on pages 90–93 to review our favorite methods for casting on, working edges, increasing and decreasing, and much more.

FINISHING

For best results, we suggest that you follow our instructions for finishing techniques. This includes seams, blocking, and the order in which the garment should be put together. If the pattern does not have specific instructions for the seam, you can choose a suitable seam from our technique section on pages 91–92.

Elongated-Neck Tunic 9

Funnel-Neck Sleeveless Top 15

Little Flirt Skirt 19

Strapped-Around Purse 21

CITY LIFE

Red Ripple-Effect Scarf 25

Red Waves Beret 27

Sleek-Line Sweater 29

Messenger Bag 33

Handsome Satchel 35

Bohemian Beret 38

Black and Gray Mélange Scarf 41

ELONGATED-NECK TUNIC

Knit in the round up to the neckline, this close-fit tunic is relatively easy to make and flatters nearly all figure types. While it maintains a career look, paired with our Little Flirt Skirt and a dressy camisole it takes on a look of utter elegance. The elongated cowl collar is gracefully draped around the neckline and the beautiful, definitive ribbing pattern on the sleeves, the bottom edge, and the collar is eyecatching.

Skill Level: Intermediate
◼◼◼◻

SIZE

To Fit Women's Size: XS (S, M, L, 1X, 2X)

Finished Bust: 34½ (37¼, 40¾, 43½, 47¼, 49¾)"

Finished Length: 29½ (30½, 31½, 32¼, 32¾, 33½)"

Finished Sleeve Length to Underarm: 17½ (18, 18, 18½, 18½, 19)"

MATERIALS

Yarn: 14 (16, 18, 20, 23, 25) balls of Cashsoft Aran from RY Classic Collection (57% extra-fine merino, 33% microfibre, 10% cashmere; 50 g; 87 m/95 yds), color SH014

Needles: US 7 (4.5 mm), US 9 (5.5 mm), US 10 (6 mm), and US 10½ (6.5 mm) circular (24" to 29"), or sizes required to obtain gauge

Notions:
2 stitch markers (different colors)

4 stitch holders

Tapestry needle

GAUGE

18 sts and 26 rows = 4" in St st (in the round), using size 9 needles

STITCH PATTERNS

C2F (cross 2 front): Sk first st on left-hand needle, knit second st through back loop. Do not remove worked st from needle. Knit the skipped st through the front. Sl both sts off needle.

Ribbing with a Twist (in the round)
(Multiple of 7 sts)

Rnd 1: *P2, K1, P2, K2; rep from * to end of rnd.

Rnd 2: *P2, K1, P2, C2F; rep from * to end of rnd.

Rep rnds 1 and 2.

Ribbing with a Twist (flat)
(Multiple of 7 sts + 1 st)

Row 1 (WS): Sl 1 wyif, *K2, P2, K2, P1; rep from * to last 7 sts, K2, P2, K2, K1tbl.

Row 2: Sl 1 wyif, *P2, C2F, P2, K1; rep from * to last 7 sts, P2, C2F, P2, K1tbl.

Rep rows 1 and 2.

Stockinette Stitch (in the round)
Knit every rnd.

Stockinette Stitch (flat)
Row 1: Knit.

Row 2: Purl.

Rep rows 1 and 2.

BODY

Using size 7 needle, CO 154 (168, 182, 196, 210, 224) sts loosely. PM, join into rnd, taking care not to twist CO row.

Work in ribbing with a twist (in the round) for 2¼ (2¼, 2¼, 2¼, 2½, 2½)".

Change to size 9 needle.

Cont in patt until piece measures 3¼ (3¼, 3¼, 3¼, 3½, 3½)" from CO edge. End after working rnd 1 as you inc 2 (0, 2, 0, 2, 0) sts evenly on this last rnd—156 (168, 184, 196, 212, 224) sts.

Knit 78 (84, 92, 98, 106, 112) sts, PM (different color) to mark side, knit to end of rnd.

Work in St st (in the round) until piece measures 15½ (16, 16½, 17, 17, 17½)" from CO edge.

Neck Shaping

Knit left front 37 (40, 44, 47, 51, 54) sts, BO 4 sts. Knit across right front to marker, knit across back to next marker, and knit left front 37 (40, 44, 47, 51, 54) sts—152 (164, 180, 192, 208, 220) sts. Turn, work sts back and forth in St st.

Purl 1 row.

Row 1: Sl 1 wyif, K1, K2tog, knit to last 4 sts, ssk, K1, K1tbl.

Rows 2, 4, and 6 (WS): Sl 1 wyif, purl to last st, K1tbl.

Rows 3 and 5: Sl 1 wyif, knit to last st, K1tbl.

Rep these 6 rows 13 (14, 15, 15, 16, 16) times. AT THE SAME TIME divide front and back when piece measures 21½ (22, 22½, 23, 23, 23½)" from CO row and ending after working WS row.

Divide for Front and Back

Work until 4 (4, 6, 6, 8, 8) sts before marker. Place sts for right front on holder. BO 8 (8, 12, 12, 16, 16) sts. Work until 4 (4, 6, 6, 8, 8) sts before next marker. Place 70 (76, 80, 86, 90, 96) sts for back on holder. BO 8 (8, 12, 12, 16, 16) sts. Work rem sts for left front.

Working both front sides at once, cont neck shaping as above. AT THE SAME TIME shape armhole.

RIGHT FRONT

Armhole Shaping

Join yarn at neck edge. Knit sts from holder. Purl 1 row.

Row 1 (RS): Knit to last 3 sts, ssk, K1.

Row 2: Purl.

Rep rows 1 and 2 for 3 (4, 4, 6, 6, 8) more times. Work even until armhole measures 7 (7½, 8, 8¼, 8¾, 9)"—15 (16, 17, 18, 19, 20) sts.

End after working WS row.

Shoulder Shaping

See page 93 for short rows technique.

Row 1 (RS): K10 (11, 12, 13, 14, 15) sts, wrap and turn.

Rows 2, 4, and 6: Purl.

Row 3: K6 (7, 8, 8, 9, 10) sts, wrap and turn.

Row 5: K2 (3, 4, 3, 4, 5) sts, wrap and turn.

Row 7: Knit. (PU wraps as you come to them)—15 (16, 17, 18, 19, 20) sts.

Place sts on holder.

LEFT FRONT

Armhole Shaping

Purl 1 row.

Row 1 (RS): K1, K2tog, knit to end of row.

Row 2: Purl.

Rep rows 1 and 2 for 3 (4, 4, 6, 6, 8) more times. Work even until armhole measures 7 (7½, 8, 8¼, 8¾, 9)"—15 (16, 17, 18, 19, 20) sts.

End after working RS row.

Shoulder Shaping

See page 93 for short rows technique.

Row 1 (WS): P10 (11, 12, 13, 14, 15) sts, wrap and turn.

Rows 2, 4, and 6: Knit.

Row 3: P6 (7, 8, 8, 9, 10) sts, wrap and turn.

Row 5: P2 (3, 4, 3, 4, 5) sts, wrap and turn.

Row 7: Purl. (PU wraps as you come to them)—15 (16, 17, 18, 19, 20) sts.

Place sts on holder.

BACK

With WS facing you, move 70 (76, 80, 86, 90, 96) sts from holder to needle. Join yarn.

Armhole Shaping

Purl 1 row.

Row 1 (RS): K1, K2tog, knit to last 3 sts, ssk, K1.

Row 2: Purl.

Rep rows 1 and 2 for 4 (5, 5, 7, 7, 9) more times. Work even until armhole measures 7 (7½, 8, 8¼, 8¾, 9)"—60 (64, 68, 70, 74, 76) sts.

End after working WS row.

Shoulder Shaping

See page 93 for short rows technique.

Row 1 (RS): K55 (59, 63, 65, 69, 71) sts, wrap and turn.

Row 2: P50 (54, 58, 60, 64, 66) sts, wrap and turn.

Row 3: K46 (50, 54, 55, 60, 61) sts, wrap and turn.

Row 4: P42 (46, 50, 50, 56, 56) sts, wrap and turn.

Row 5: K38 (42, 46, 45, 50, 51) sts, wrap and turn.

Row 6: P34 (38, 42, 40, 44, 46) sts, wrap and turn.

Row 7: K47 (51, 55, 55, 59, 61) sts (PU wraps as you come to them).

Row 8: P15 (16, 17, 18, 19, 20) sts, BO 30 (32, 34, 34, 36, 36) sts, purl rem sts (PU wraps as you come to them).

Place shoulder sts on holder.

The ribbing pattern is a combination of a simple ribbing and a twist.

SLEEVE (Make 2)

Using size 7 needle, CO 43 (43, 50, 50, 57, 57) sts.

Work in ribbing with a twist (flat) until piece measures 4½" from CO edge.

Change to size 9 needle.

Cont in patt until 6" from CO edge.

End after working WS row.

Work even in St st (flat) for 7 (5, 7, 7, 7, 3) rows.

Inc row: Sl 1 wyif, incR, knit to last st, incL, K1tbl.

Rep inc row every 6 rows 0 (1, 0, 5, 0, 12) times, every 8 rows 6 (7, 5, 4, 4, 0) times, and every 10 rows 1 (0, 2, 0, 3, 0) times—59 (61, 66, 70, 73, 83) sts.

Work even until sleeve measures 17½ (18, 18, 18½, 18½, 19)" from CO edge, end after working WS row.

Shape cap: BO 4 (4, 6, 6, 8, 8) sts at beg of next 2 rows.

Dec 1 st at each end of EOR 6 (6, 7, 8, 8, 7) times, every 4 rows 1 time, EOR 4 (5, 7, 7, 8, 7) times, and every row 9 (8, 5, 5, 3, 9) times. BO rem 11 (13, 14, 16, 17, 19) sts.

FINISHING

Block all pieces, using method 1 on page 93. Join shoulders, using 3-needle BO (see page 91). Sew side seams.

Collar

With WS facing you, using size 7 needle, and beg at left front shoulder, PU 30 (32, 34, 34, 36, 36) sts across back neck, 95 (94, 96, 96, 99, 99) sts along right neck edge, 4 sts at neck BO, and 95 (94, 97, 97, 99, 99) sts along left neck edge to left shoulder—224 (224, 231, 231, 238, 238) sts. PM, join into rnd.

Work ribbing with a twist (in the round) for 7 rnds.

Change to size 9 needle and work 9 more rnds.

Change to size 10 needle and work 9 more rnds.

Change to size 10½ needle and work 4 more rnds.

BO all sts loosely in patt.

Sew sleeve seams beg at ribbing (CO edge), using flat stitch seam (see page 91). Cont to sew sleeve seams above ribbing using mattress st, vertical stockinette st (see page 92). Sew sleeves into armholes. Work in all ends. Block finished garment, using method 1 on page 93.

Ribbing with a Twist (in the round)
Multiple of 7 sts

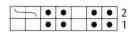

In the round, all rows in the chart are worked from right to left.

Ribbing with a Twist (flat)
Multiple of 7 sts + 1 st

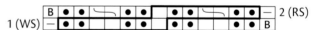

Key

☐ K on RS, P on WS
● P on RS, K on WS
− Sl 1 st purlwise wyif
B K1 tbl
⟍ C2F: Sk first st and knit 2nd st in back loop, then knit skipped st in front loop; sl both sts from needle

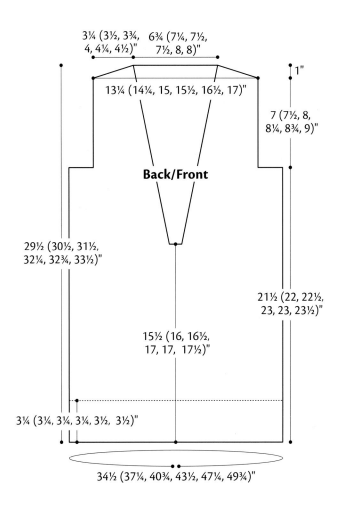

3¼ (3½, 3¾, 4, 4¼, 4½)"   6¾ (7¼, 7½, 7½, 8, 8)"

13¼ (14¼, 15, 15½, 16½, 17)"

1"

Back/Front

7 (7½, 8, 8¼, 8¾, 9)"

29½ (30½, 31½, 32¼, 32¾, 33½)"

21½ (22, 22½, 23, 23, 23½)"

15½ (16, 16½, 17, 17, 17½)"

3¼ (3¼, 3¼, 3¼, 3½, 3½)"

34½ (37¼, 40¾, 43½, 47¼, 49¾)"

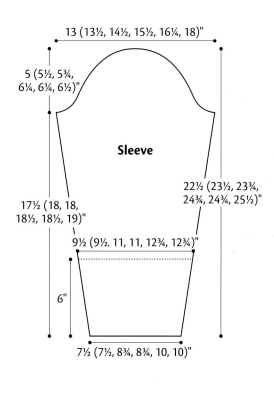

13 (13½, 14½, 15½, 16¼, 18)"

5 (5½, 5¾, 6¼, 6¼, 6½)"

Sleeve

22½ (23½, 23¾, 24¾, 24¾, 25½)"

17½ (18, 18, 18½, 18½, 19)"

9½ (9½, 11, 11, 12¾, 12¾)"

6"

7½ (7½, 8¾, 8¾, 10, 10)"

FUNNEL-NECK SLEEVELESS TOP

While this dressy sleeveless top serves as a background for our Elongated-Neck Tunic, it can easily bring drama to any outfit on its own. Simple, classic lines allow for a scene change from work to play.

Skill Level: Easy ◖■☐☐

SIZE

To Fit Women's Size: XS (S, M, L)

Finished Bust: 34½ (36, 39, 41¾)"

Finished Length to Back Neck: 20¼ (21, 22, 22½)"

MATERIALS

Yarn: 3 (4, 5, 6) balls of Dolly by Bollicine from Cascade Yarns (100% merino wool extra fine shrink resistant; 50 g/1.76 oz; 153 yds/140 m), color 705 (**3**)

Needles: US 5 (3.75 mm) and US 6 (4 mm) circular (29"), and US 5 and US 6 circular (16"), or sizes required to obtain gauge

Notions:
2 stitch holders

Stitch marker

Tapestry needle

GAUGE

22 sts and 28 rows = 4" in St st, using size 6 needles

26 sts and 28 rows = 4" in 1 x 1 ribbing, using size 5 needles

STITCH PATTERNS

Stockinette Stitch (in the round)

Knit every rnd.

Stockinette Stitch (flat)

Row 1: Knit.

Row 2: Purl.

Rep rows 1 and 2.

1 x 1 Ribbing

(Even number of sts)

All rnds: *P1, K1; rep from * to end of rnd.

BODY

Garment is worked in the round. When finished, purl side is used as right side.

Using 29" size 5 needle, CO 190 (198, 214, 230) sts. PM, join into rnd, taking care not to twist CO row.

Work in 1 x 1 ribbing for a total of 7 rnds.

Change to 29" size 6 needle. Work in following patt: K44 (46, 50, 54), (P1, K1) 3 times, P1, K139 (145, 157, 169) until piece measures 8½, (9, 9, 9)".

Work underarm ribbing as follows:

Rnds 1–3: P1, K43 (45, 49, 53), (P1, K1) 3 times, P1, K43 (45, 49, 53), P2, K93 (97, 105, 113), P1.

Rnds 4–6: P1, K1, P1, K41 (43, 47, 51), (P1, K1) 3 times, P1, K41 (43, 47, 51), P1, K1, P2, K1, P1, K89 (93, 101, 109), P1, K1, P1.

Rnds 7–9: P1, (K1, P1) 2 times, K39 (41, 45, 49), (P1, K1) 3 times, P1, K39 (41, 45, 49), (P1, K1) 2 times, P2, (K1, P1) 2 times, K85 (89, 97, 105), (P1, K1) 2 times, P1.

Rnds 10–12: P1, (K1, P1) 3 times, K37 (39, 43, 47), (P1, K1) 3 times, P1, K37 (39, 43, 47), (P1, K1) 3 times, P2, (K1, P1) 3 times, K81 (85, 93, 101), (P1, K1) 3 times, P1.

Rnds 13–15: P1, (K1, P1) 4 times, K35 (37, 41, 45), (P1, K1) 3 times, P1, K35 (37, 41, 45), (P1, K1) 4 times, P2, (K1, P1) 4 times, K77 (81, 89, 97), (P1, K1) 4 times, P1.

Rnds 16–18: P1, (K1, P1) 5 times, K33 (35, 39, 43), (P1, K1) 3 times, P1, K33 (35, 39, 43), (P1, K1) 5 times, P2, (K1, P1) 5 times, K73 (77, 85, 93), (P1, K1) 5 times, P1.

Rnds 19–21: P1, (K1, P1) 6 times, K31 (33, 37, 41), (P1, K1) 3 times, P1, K31 (33, 37, 41), (P1, K1) 6 times, P2, (K1, P1) 6 times, K69 (73, 81, 89), (P1, K1) 6 times, P1.

Rnds 22–24: P1, (K1, P1) 7 times, K29 (31, 35, 39), (P1, K1) 3 times, P1, K29 (31, 35, 39), (P1, K1) 7 times, P2, (K1, P1) 7 times, K65 (69, 77, 85), (P1, K1) 7 times, P1.

Rnds 25–27: P1, (K1, P1) 8 times, K27 (29, 33, 37), (P1, K1) 3 times, P1, K27 (29, 33, 37), (P1, K1) 8 times, P2, (K1, P1) 8 times, K61 (65, 73, 81), (P1, K1) 8 times, P1.

Rnd 28: P1, (K1, P1) 9 times, K25 (27, 31, 35), (P1, K1) 3 times, P1, K25 (27, 31, 35), (P1, K1) 9 times, P2, (K1, P1) 9 times, K57 (61, 69, 77), (P1, K1) 9 times, P1.

For sizes XS and S only:

Rep rnd 28 until piece measures 13½ (14)" from CO edge. Beg armhole shaping.

For sizes M and L only:

Rnds 29 and 30: Rep rnd 28.

Rnd 31: P1, (K1, P1) 10 times, K29 (33), (P1, K1) 3 times, P1, K29 (33), (P1, K1) 10 times, P2, (K1, P1) 10 times, K65 (73), (P1, K1) 10 times, P1.

Rep rnd 31 until piece measures 14½ (14½)" from CO edge. Beg armhole shaping.

Armhole Shaping

For armhole only, BO sts in patt with firm tension.

Work in est patt across 179 (187, 201, 217) sts, BO 11 (11, 13, 13) sts before marker, and 11 (11, 13, 13) sts after marker, P1, (K1, P1) 3 times, K25 (27, 29, 33), (P1, K1) 3 times, P1, K25 (27, 29, 33), (P1, K1) 4 times, BO 22 (22, 26, 26) sts, P1, (K1, P1) 3 times, K57 (61, 65, 73), (P1, K1) 4 times—146 (154, 162, 178) sts.

Place 73 (77, 81, 89) front sts on holder.

BACK

Work 73 (77, 81, 89) sts as follows:

Row 1: Sl 1 wyif, (K1, P1) 3 times, K1, purl to last 8 sts, (K1, P1) 3 times, sl 1 wyib, K1tbl.

Row 2: Sl 1 wyif, (P1, K1) 3 times, P1, knit to last 8 sts, (P1, K1) 3 times, sl 1 wyif, K1tbl.

Rep rows 1 and 2 until armhole measures 6¾ (7, 7½, 8)". BO 20 (21, 22, 25) sts for shoulder in patt, place 33 (35, 37, 39) sts on holder for back neck, and BO 20 (21, 22, 25) sts for other shoulder in patt.

FRONT

Move 73 (77, 81, 89) front sts from holder onto needle.

Work same as for back until armhole measures 4¾ (5, 5¼, 5¾)".

Divide for Neck and Shoulders

Sl 1 wyif, (P1, K1) 3 times, P1, K14 (16, 18, 21), K2tog, K1, place next 23 (23, 23, 25) sts on holder, join second ball of yarn, K1, ssk, K14 (16, 18, 21), (P1, K1) 3 times, sl 1 wyif, K1tbl.

Work left and right sides of front at the same time on 24 (26, 28, 31) sts each.

Right Neck and Shoulder

Row 1: Sl 1 wyif, (K1, P1) 3 times, K1, purl to last st, K1tbl.

Row 2: Sl 1 wyif, ssk, knit to last 8 sts, (P1, K1) 3 times, sl 1 wyif, K1tbl.

Rep rows 1 and 2 for a total of 4 (5, 6, 6) times—20 (21, 22, 25) sts.

Work even until armhole measures 6¾ (7, 7½, 8)". BO all sts in patt.

Left Neck and Shoulder

Row 1: Sl 1 wyif, purl to last 8 sts, (K1, P1) 3 times, sl 1 wyib, K1tbl.

Row 2: Sl 1 wyif, (P1, K1) 3 times, P1, knit to last 3 sts, K2tog, K1tbl.

Rep rows 1 and 2 for a total of 4 (5, 6, 6) times—20 (21, 22, 25) sts.

Work even until armhole measures 6¾ (7, 7½, 8)". BO all sts in patt.

FINISHING

Block, using method 1 on page 93, before sewing shoulder seams. Do not stretch ribbed areas. Turn garment purl-side out (RS). Sew shoulder seams.

Neck

With RS facing you, beg at left shoulder. Using 16" size 5 needle, join yarn, PU 12 (13, 14, 15) sts along left front neck, K23 (23, 23, 25) sts from neck holder, PU 12 (13, 14, 15) sts along right front neck, K33 (35, 37, 39) sts from back holder, PM, join into rnd—80 (84, 88, 94) sts.

Rnd 1: *K1, P1; rep from * to end of rnd.

Rep rnd 1 until neck measures 2½".

Change to 16" size 6 needle.

Work for 1" more. BO all sts in patt loosely.

Work in all ends. Block garment again, using method 1 on page 93. Do not stretch ribbed areas.

Funnel neck is done in ribbing pattern for close fit. Strategically placed ribbing pattern takes care of armhole finishing as you knit it.

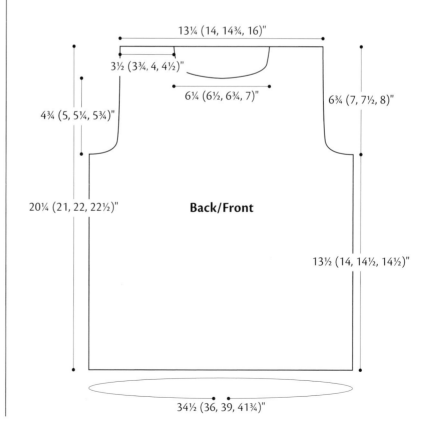

13¼ (14, 14¾, 16)"

3½ (3¾, 4, 4½)"

6¼ (6½, 6¾, 7)"

6¾ (7, 7½, 8)"

4¾ (5, 5¼, 5¾)"

20¼ (21, 22, 22½)"

Back/Front

13½ (14, 14½, 14½)"

34½ (36, 39, 41¾)"

In a busy city life, this skirt can add flirt to your daytime or evening wear. The straight body with flirty pleats at the bottom makes this skirt slimming and flattering for most figure types. The elastic waistband allows for a custom fit. Because it's knit in the round in simple stitch patterns, it's an easy project to knit. This skirt will quickly become a wardrobe favorite.

Skill Level: Intermediate

SIZE

To Fit Women's Size: XS (S, M, L, 1X, 2X)

Finished Waist (Excluding Elastic): 27¾ (29¼, 32, 34¾, 37½, 40¼)"

Finished Hip: 38¼ (40, 44, 48, 52, 56)"

Finished Length: 22½ (23, 23½, 24, 24½, 25)"

MATERIALS

Yarn: 3 (4, 4, 5, 5, 6) skeins of Cascade 220 (100% Peruvian Highland wool; 100 g/3.5 oz; 220 yds), color 8555

Needles: US 5 (3.75 mm), US 7 (4.5 mm), US 8 (5 mm), US 9 (5.5 mm), and US 10 (6 mm) circular (24" to 29"), or sizes required to obtain gauge

Notions:
1¼ yards of 1"-wide nonrolling elastic for waistband

Stitch marker

Tapestry needle

GAUGE

All gauges are given for knitting in the round.

16 sts and 22 rows = 4" in 7 x 6 ribbing (slightly stretched), using size 10 needles

18 sts and 26 rows = 4" in St st (in the round), using size 8 needles

23 sts and 28 rows = 4" in 1 x 1 ribbing (slightly stretched), using size 5 needles

STITCH PATTERNS

Stockinette Stitch (in the round)
Knit every rnd.

7 x 6 Ribbing
(Multiple of 13 sts)

All rnds: *K7, P6; rep from * to end of rnd.

1 x 1 Ribbing
(Even number of sts)

All rnds: *K1, P1; rep from * to end of rnd.

PLEATS

Using size 10 needle, CO 247 (260, 286, 312, 338, 364) sts. PM, join into rnd, taking care not to twist CO row.

Rnds 1 and 3: Knit.

Rnds 2 and 4: Purl.

Work 7 x 6 ribbing as follows:

Rnds 5–15: *K7, P6; rep from * to end of rnd.

Rnd 16: *K7, P2, P2tog, P2; rep from * to end of rnd—228 (240, 264, 288, 312, 336) sts.

Rnds 17–20: *K7, P5; rep from * to end of rnd.

Rnd 21: *K7, P2, P2tog, P1; rep from * to end of rnd—209 (220, 242, 264, 286, 308) sts.

Rnds 22–27: *K7, P4; rep from * to end of rnd.

Rnd 28: *K7, P1, P2tog, P1; rep from * to end of rnd—190 (200, 220, 240, 260, 280) sts.

Rnds 29–34: *K7, P3; rep from * to end of rnd.

Rnd 35: *K7, P1, P2tog; rep from * to end of rnd—171 (180, 198, 216, 234, 252) sts.

Rnds 36–44: *K7, P2; rep from * to end of rnd.

For size XS only:

Inc 1 st on the last rnd—172 sts.

EYELET BORDER

Change to size 9 needle.

Rnds 1, 3, 5, and 7: Purl.

Rnds 2 and 6: Knit.

Rnd 4: *YO, K2tog; rep from * to end of rnd.

SKIRT BODY

Work in St st for 3 (3, 3, 4, 4, 4)".

Change to size 8 needle and cont in St st until skirt measures 20 (20½, 21, 21½, 22, 22½)".

Change to size 7 needle.

For sizes S, M, L only:

Knit 7 rnds.

For sizes 1X and 2X only:

Dec rnd: K2tog, K115 (124), K2tog, K115 (124)—232 (250) sts.

Knit 6 rnds.

For all sizes:

Dec rnd: *K41 (43, 31, 25, 27, 23), K2tog; rep from * to end of rnd—168 (176, 192, 208, 224, 240) sts.

WAISTBAND

Change to size 5 needle.

Work 1 x 1 ribbing as follows:

Rnds 1–9: *K1, P1; rep from * to end of rnd.

Rnd 10 (turning rnd): Purl.

Rnds 11–15: Knit.

Rnd 16 (dec rnd): *K19 (20, 22, 24, 26, 28), K2tog; rep from * to end of rnd—160 (168, 184, 200, 216, 232) sts.

Rnds 17 and 18: Knit.

BO all sts.

FINISHING

Weave in all ends. Block skirt, using method 1 on page 93.

Waistband: Cut elastic 1½" less than actual waist measurement. Fold waistband along turning rnd to inside of skirt and stitch bind-off edge to rnd 1, leaving 1" opening. Insert elastic; sew ends together securely. Stitch opening and block waistband again.

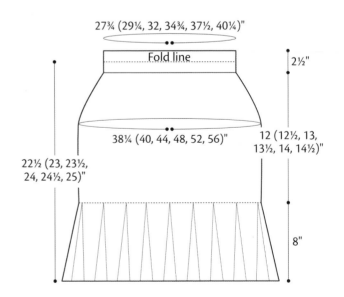

27¾ (29¼, 32, 34¾, 37½, 40¼)"

Fold line

2½"

38¼ (40, 44, 48, 52, 56)"

12 (12½, 13, 13½, 14, 14½)"

22½ (23, 23½, 24, 24½, 25)"

8"

If you can make a hat, you can make this felted purse. It is a great size for being on the go or for a casual evening. The rolled-edge shoulder strap holds the shape of the bag as well as adds a decorative touch. The inside pocket creates order for your contents.

Skill Level: Intermediate

◼◼◼◻

SIZE (After Felting)

Finished Body Diameter: approx 10½"

Finished Length: approx 23½" (shoulder to bottom of purse)

MATERIALS

Yarn: Cascade 220 (100% Peruvian Highland wool; 100 g/3.5 oz; 220 yds) (4)

   A: 3 skeins of color 4002

   B: 1 skein of color 8400

Needles: US 11 (8 mm) circular (32") and US 11 double-pointed needles, or size required to obtain gauge

Notions:

6 removable stitch markers

Stitch marker

Magnetic snap

Heavy-duty thread and sewing needle

One 1½"-diameter button

Tapestry needle

Stiff brush or Slicker Brush (available at pet stores)

GAUGE

Gauge is given for knitting in the round before felting.

11 sts and 13 rows = 4" in St st with 2 strands of yarn held tog

STITCH PATTERN

Stockinette Stitch (in the round)

Knit every rnd.

Note: Use 2 strands of yarn held tog throughout unless otherwise instructed.

FRONT/BACK (Make 1 of each)

Using circular needle and A, CO 130 sts. PM, join into rnd, taking care not to twist CO row.

Rnd 1: Purl.

Rnd 2: Knit.

Work dec rnds as follows, changing to dpns when necessary.

Rnd 3: *K11, K2tog; rep from * to end of rnd—120 sts.

Rnds 4, 5, 7, 8, 10, 11, 13, 14, 16, 17, and 19–29 odd: Knit.

Rnd 6: *K10, ssk; rep from * to end of rnd—110 sts.

Rnd 9: *K9, K2tog; rep from * to end of rnd—100 sts.

Rnd 12: *K8, ssk; rep from * to end of rnd—90 sts.

Rnd 15: *K7, K2tog; rep from * to end of rnd—80 sts.

Rnd 18: *K6, ssk; rep from * to end of rnd—70 sts.

Rnd 20: *K5, K2tog; rep from * to end of rnd—60 sts.

Rnd 22: *K4, ssk; rep from * to end of rnd—50 sts.

Rnd 24: *K3, K2tog; rep from * to end of rnd—40 sts.

Rnd 26: *K2, ssk; rep from * to end of rnd—30 sts.

Rnd 28: *K1, K2tog; rep from * to end of rnd—20 sts.

Rnd 30: Ssk to end of rnd—10 sts.

Rnd 31: K2tog to end of rnd—5 sts.

Pull yarn through rem 5 sts and draw up tightly. Weave tail loosely to knit side. Mark purl side of each circle as RS.

Each piece is a circle with 10 wedges. Referring to diagram at right, place a removable marker at point C. Count 7 wedges and place a removable marker at point D (see diagram on page 23).

GUSSET/STRAP

Using circular needle and B, CO 165 sts. PM, join into rnd, taking care not to twist CO row.

Rnds 1–5: Purl with B.

Rnds 6–11: Knit with A.

Rnd 12: Knit with B.

Rnds 13–16: Purl with B.

BO all sts.

To lengthen or shorten strap, add or subtract sts at CO: 4 sts = 1" in felted length.

POCKET

Using circular needle and A, CO 30 sts.

Rows 1–12: Knit with A.

Rows 13–16: Knit with B.

Rows 17–22: Knit with A.

Rows 23–26: Knit with B.

Rows 27–38: Knit with A.

BO all sts.

FINISHING

Strap

Allow the CO and BO edges to roll to WS. With WS facing you and 1 strand B, sew each st from CO edge to each st of rnd 5, using overcast st (see page 92). This creates rolled edge on strap. Take care not to pull tightly. Sew BO edge to rnd 12 in same manner.

Attach Strap to Purse

With RS facing you, place front of purse inside of strap. Place removable markers E and F on the strap to match points C and D on the purse. Use overcast st (see page 92) and 1 strand A to sew 7 wedges of front to strap from C to D in counterclockwise direction. Sewing is done from RS of purse to WS of strap at rolled edge seam. Take care not to pull tightly. Rolled edge of strap will position itself on top of purse. Make a second seam from C to D in counterclockwise direction, sewing the top of rolled edge to front of purse (approx ¼" outside of first seam). This opens gusset of purse. Reinforce C to E and D to F (see diagram at right). Rep for back of purse.

Felting

Felt both purse and pocket according to "Felting" instructions on page 93. Place purse on flat surface. To ensure circular shape, smooth and flatten front and back.

Finishing Touches

When dried completely, cut across top of front from C to D (see diagram at right) to form straight edge. Fold top of back to form flap. Attach magnetic snap. Using sewing needle and heavy-duty thread, sew button to cover snap.

Turn purse to WS. Stitch pocket on back of purse below flap. Turn purse to RS. Brush surface with stiff brush. Trim any excess fuzz and yarn tails.

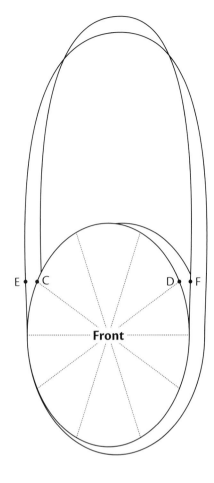

The main feature of this bag is the continuous strap that encloses the purse body and serves as a gusset.

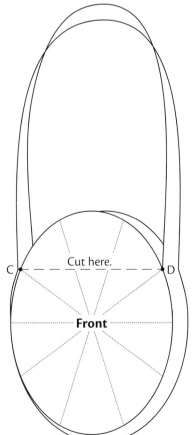

RED RIPPLE-EFFECT SCARF

Complete your outfit with this distinctive scarf. It will keep you warm and make you feel in vogue; soft and rich alpaca yarn brings character to this cozy scarf. The pattern is an easy one-row repeat that produces a lovely ripple effect.

Skill Level: Intermediate

SIZE

Finished Measurements: Approx 5¾" x 62" (excluding fringe)

MATERIALS

Yarn: 2 skeins of Ultra Alpaca from Berroco (50% alpaca, 50% wool; 100 g/3.5 oz; 215 yds/198 m), color 6234 ▣

Needles: US 10½ (6.5 mm), or size required to obtain gauge

Notions:
Size I-9 (5.5 mm) crochet hook

GAUGE

18 sts = 4" in patt; row gauge is not important for this scarf

SCARF

YO is not counted as a separate st in this patt.

CO 26 sts.

Row 1: Sl 1 wyif, *YO, sl 1 wyib, K1tbl; rep from * to last st, K1tbl.

Row 2: Sl 1 wyif, *YO, sl 1 wyib, then knit YO from previous row tog with next st tbl; rep from * to last st, K1tbl.

Rep row 2 until scarf measures 62". BO as you work following patt: sl 1 wyif, *sl 1 wyib, knit YO from previous row tog with next st tbl; rep from * to last st, K1tbl.

FRINGE

Cut 72 pieces of yarn, 12" long (36 for each end of scarf). Using crochet hook and 3 strands of yarn, attach 12 fringes at each end of scarf.

FINISHING

Work in all ends. Block scarf, using method 1 on page 93. Trim fringe even.

Detail of reversible stitch pattern

Look trendy while staying warm as you wear this timeless beret. It is knit in the round. The feminine and gentle look of this hat is accomplished by a combination of the stitch pattern and the decorative cast on.

Skill Level: Intermediate

SIZE: One Size

Finished Circumference: Approx 21¼"

MATERIALS

Yarn: 1 skein of Ultra Alpaca from Berroco (50% alpaca, 50% wool; 100 g/3.5 oz; 215 yds/ 198 m), color 6234 (4)

Needles: US 4 (3.5 mm) and US 8 (5 mm) circular (16" to 20"), and US 8 double-pointed, or sizes required to obtain gauge, and US 11 (8 mm) straight (used for CO only)

Notions:

11 stitch markers

Tapestry needle

GAUGE

All gauges are given for knitting in the round.

20 sts and 45 rows = 4" in slip stitch ribbing, using size 4 needles

16 sts and 21 rows = 4" in little waves patt, using size 8 needles

STITCH PATTERNS

Slip-Stitch Ribbing

(Even number of sts)

Rnd 1: *K1, P1; rep from * to end of rnd.

Rnd 2: Knit.

Rnd 3: *Sl 1 wyib, P1; rep from * to end of rnd.

Rep rnds 2 and 3.

Little Waves

(Odd number of sts)

Rnd 1: *YO, P2, pass YO over 2 purled sts; rep from * to last st, P1.

Rnd 2: Knit.

Rnd 3: P1, *YO, P2, pass YO over 2 purled sts; rep from * to end of rnd.

Rep rnds 1–3.

BAND

Using size 11 needle, CO 106 sts using decorative cast-on method on page 90.

Switch to size 4 needle, work rnd 1 of slip-st ribbing. PM, join into rnd, taking care not to twist CO row. Marker indicates center back.

Work in slip-st ribbing for a total of 14 rnds, ending with rnd 2.

BODY

Change to size 8 needle.

Inc rnd: K1, *P2, K1f&b in the next st; rep from * to end of rnd—141 sts.

Work in little waves patt for 19 rnds.

CROWN SHAPING

Work decs as follows, changing to dpns when necessary.

Rnd 1: K6, K2tog, PM, (K12, K2tog, PM) 9 times, K7, PM—131 sts.

Rnd 2: (YO, P2, pass YO over 2 purled sts) 3 times, P1, *(YO, P2, pass YO over 2 purled sts) 6 times, P1; rep from * 8 more times, (YO, P2, pass YO over 2 purled sts) 3 times, P1.

Rnd 3: Knit.

Rnd 4: P1, (YO, P2, pass YO over 2 purled sts) 3 times, *P1, (YO, P2, pass YO over 2 purled sts) 6 times; rep from * 8 more times, P1, (YO, P2, pass YO over 2 purled sts) 3 times.

Rnd 5: K5, K2tog, (K11, K2tog) 9 times, K5, K2tog—120 sts.

Rnd 6: *YO, P2, pass YO over 2 purled sts; rep from * to end of rnd.

Rnd 7: K4, K2tog, (K10, K2tog) 9 times, K4, K2tog—109 sts.

Rnd 8: P1, (YO, P2, pass YO over 2 purled sts) 2 times, *P1, (YO, P2, pass YO over 2 purled sts) 5 times; rep from * 8 more times, P1, (YO, P2, pass YO over 2 purled sts) 2 times.

Rnd 9: K3, K2tog, (K9, K2tog) 9 times, K3, K2tog—98 sts.

Rnd 10: *YO, P2, pass YO over 2 purled sts; rep from * to end of rnd.

Rnd 11: K2, K2tog, (K8, K2tog) 9 times, K2, K2tog—87 sts.

Rnd 12: P1, YO, P2, pass YO over 2 purled sts, *P1, (YO, P2, pass YO over 2 purled sts) 4 times; rep from * 8 more times, P1, YO, P2, pass YO over 2 purled sts.

Rnd 13: K1, K2tog, (K7, K2tog) 9 times, K1, K2tog—76 sts.

Rnd 14: *YO, P2, pass YO over 2 purled sts; rep from * to end of rnd.

Rnd 15: K2tog, (K6, K2tog) 9 times, K2tog—65 sts.

Rnd 16: P1, (YO, P2, pass YO over 2 purled sts) 4 times, *P1, (YO, P2, pass YO over 2 purled sts) 3 times; rep from * 7 more times.

Rnd 17: K6, K2tog, (K5, K2tog) 8 times, K1—56 sts.

Rnd 18: *P1, (YO, P2, pass YO over 2 purled sts) 3 times; rep from * 7 more times.

Rnd 19: K5, K2tog, (K4, K2tog) 8 times, K1—47 sts.

Rnd 20: (YO, P2, pass YO over 2 purled sts) 3 times, (YO, P2, pass YO over 2 purled sts, YO, P1, P2tog, pass YO over 2 purled sts) 7 times, (YO, P2, pass YO over 2 purled sts) 3 times—40 sts.

Rnd 21: K4, K2tog, (K2, K2tog) 7 times, K4, K2tog—31 sts.

Rnd 22: YO, P2, pass YO over 2 purled sts, (YO, P1, P2tog, pass YO over 2 purled sts) 9 times, P2tog—21 sts.

Rnd 23: K1, *K2tog; rep from * to end of rnd—11 sts.

Pull yarn through rem 11 sts. Fasten securely.

FINISHING

Work in all ends. Block, using method 1 on page 93.

Detail of decorative cast on

SLEEK-LINE SWEATER

Richly textured with sleek lines, this sweater quickly becomes a favorite for a man with style. The luxury alpaca yarn makes this sweater irresistible. The corrugated pattern is complementary to the lines of this sweater.

Skill Level: Intermediate

▰▰▰▱

SIZE

To Fit Men's Size: XS (S, M, L, XL)

Finished Chest: 39 (42½, 46½, 50, 54)"

Finished Back Length: 24½ (25½, 26½, 27½, 28½)"

Finished Sleeve Length to Underarm: 17½ (18, 18½, 19, 19½)"

MATERIALS

Yarn: 8 (9, 10, 11, 12) skeins of Ultra Alpaca from Berroco (50% alpaca, 50% wool; 100 g/3.5 oz, 215 yds/198 m), color 6289 ▣

Needles: US 7 (4.5 mm) and US 8 (5 mm) straight, and US 7 circular (20"), or size required to obtain gauge

Notions:

Tapestry needle

Size F-5 (3.75 mm) crochet hook

2 yds of any matching color cotton yarn

GAUGE

26 sts and 29 rows = 4" in broken rib st, using size 7 needles

25 sts and 28 rows = 4" in broken rib st, using size 8 needles

BROKEN RIB STITCH

(Multiple of 4 sts + 3 sts, plus 2 edge sts)

Row 1 (RS): Sl 1 wyif, K2, *P2, K2; rep from * to last 2 sts, P1, K1tbl.

Row 2 (WS): Sl 1 wyif, P2 *K2, P2; rep from * to last 2 sts, K1, K1tbl.

Rep rows 1 and 2.

When dec or inc, keep edge sts and patt as est.

BACK

Using size 7 straight needles, CO 121 (133, 145, 157, 169) sts.

Work in broken rib st for a total of 16 rows.

Change to size 8 needles.

Cont working in patt until piece measures 15½ (16, 16½, 17, 17½)" from CO. End after working WS row.

Armhole Shaping

BO 6 (6, 6, 7, 8) sts at beg of next 2 rows. Dec 1 st at each end of next row, and then on EOR 3 (5, 8, 9, 11) times—101 (109, 115, 123, 129) sts rem. Work even until armhole measures 8½ (9, 9½, 10, 10½)".

Neck and Shoulder Shaping

Work 35 (38, 40, 43, 45) sts, join second ball of yarn and BO center 31 (33, 35, 37, 39) sts, work rem sts. Working both sides at the same time, dec 1 st at neck edge every row 3 (3, 4, 4, 4) times—32 (35, 36, 39, 41) sts. Work even until armhole measures 9 (9½, 10, 10½, 11)". BO all sts.

FRONT

Work as for back until armhole measures 7 (7½, 8, 8½, 9)".

Neck and Shoulder Shaping

Work 40 (43, 45, 48, 50) sts, join second ball of yarn and BO center 21 (23, 25, 27, 29) sts, work rem sts. Working both sides at the same time, dec 1 st at each neck edge every row 8 (8, 9, 9, 9) times—32 (35, 36, 39, 41) sts. Work even until armhole measures same as for back. BO all sts.

SLEEVE (Make 2)

Using size 7 straight needles, CO 57 (61, 65, 69, 73) sts.

Work in broken rib st for 8 rows.

Change to size 8 needles.

Work 8 more rows. Inc 1 st at each end of next row, then every 8 rows 8 (9, 6, 4, 3) times and every 6 rows 6 (5, 10, 13, 15) times—87 (91, 99, 105, 111) sts. Work even until sleeve measures 17½ (18, 18½, 19, 19½)".

Cap Shaping

BO 6 (6, 6, 7, 8) sts at beg of next 2 rows. Dec 1 st at each end of every row 2 (4, 9, 10, 10) times, on EOR 17 (11, 12, 12, 15) times, and then every 4 rows 1 (4, 2, 2, 1) times.

BO 4 (5, 5, 5, 5) sts at beg of next 4 rows. BO rem 19 (21, 21, 23, 23) sts.

FINISHING

Block all pieces, using method 1 on page 93. Sew shoulder seams.

Reinforce Shoulder Seams

Using crochet hook and cotton yarn, join yarn at neck edge. Working above the shoulder seam, crochet a chain through 1 st of front and 1 st of back. Rep for all sts. Fasten off. This will help support weight of sleeves.

Neck Trim

With RS facing you, using size 7 circular needle, beg at left shoulder, PU 15 (16, 19, 20, 20) sts along left front neck, 21 (23, 25, 27, 29) sts at center neck, 15 (16, 19, 20, 20) sts along right front neck, 4 (4, 4, 5, 5) sts along right back neck, 31 (33, 35, 37, 39) sts at center back neck, 4 (4, 4, 5, 5) sts along left back neck—90 (96, 106, 114, 118) sts. Work applied I-cord as follows: CO 3 sts on LH needle. Using size 7 straight needle, *K2, ssk (1 st from I-cord and 1 st from neck). Slip 3 sts back to left needle; rep from * until all sts are worked. BO rem 3 sts. Sew BO edge to CO edge.

Sew sleeve cap into armhole. Sew side and sleeve seams. Work in ends. Block finished garment, using method 1 on page 93.

Broken Rib Stitch
Multiple of 4 sts + 3 sts, plus 2 edge sts

Key

- ☐ K on RS, P on WS
- ● P on RS, K on WS
- — Sl 1 st purlwise wyif
- B K1 tbl

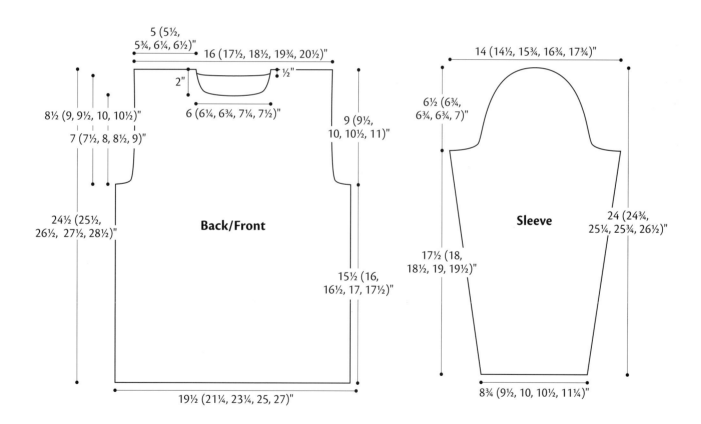

Walk around the city in style with this well-designed bag. Its size and sturdy strap make it suitable for, but not limited to, carrying a laptop. The darker of two complementary colors trims the flap and shoulder strap. The bag is an excellent accessory for a man or a woman. The appearance of this bag suggests a difficult pattern, which is deceiving. You will be pleasantly surprised by the simplicity of this project.

Skill Level: Intermediate
■■■□

SIZE (After Felting)

Finished Body Dimensions: Approx 15" wide x 13" tall x 2" deep

Finished Length: Approx 36" (shoulder to bottom of bag)

MATERIALS

Yarn: Cascade 220 from Cascade Yarns (100% Peruvian Highland wool; 100 g/3.5 oz; 220 yds) 【4】

   A: 6 skeins of color 8400

   B: 2 skeins of color 8555

Needles: US 11 (8 mm) circular (32") and US 11 (8 mm) double-pointed, or size required to obtain gauge

Notions:

Removable stitch marker

Stitch marker

Heavy-duty thread to match A, and sewing needle

Tapestry needle

One 1¾" square button

Box, 15" wide x 13" tall x 2" deep

Stiff brush or Slicker Brush (available at pet stores)

GAUGE

Gauge is given for knitting in the round before felting.

12 sts and 13 rows = 4" in St st with 2 strands of yarn held tog

STITCH PATTERNS

Stockinette Stitch (in the round)

Knit every rnd.

Stockinette Stitch (flat)

Row 1: Knit.

Row 2: Purl.

Rep rows 1 and 2.

Garter Stitch (flat)

Knit every row.

Note: Use 2 strands of yarn held tog throughout unless otherwise instructed.

BOTTOM

Using circular needle and A, CO 48 sts.

Work in garter st for 12 rows. Do not turn.

BODY

With 48 sts on needle, PU 11 sts along short side of bottom (gusset); PU 48 sts along CO edge; PU 11 sts on other short side (gusset)—118 sts.

PM, join into rnd.

Rnd 1: K48, sl 1 wyib, K9, sl 1 wyib, K48, sl 1 wyib, K9, sl 1 wyib.

Rnd 2: Knit.

Rep these 2 rnds until piece measures 18" from PU rnd. End after working rnd 2.

K48, place removable marker in next st. BO next 70 sts with firm tension—48 sts.

FLAP

Working back and forth on 48 sts, knit 2 rows. Purl next row (RS).

Work in St st for 16". End after working a purl row. BO all sts with firm tension.

TRIM

Using B and beg at removable marker, PU 11 sts across gusset, 48 sts across front, 11 sts across other gusset, 3 sts for every 4 rows on long side of flap, 48 sts across end of flap, and 3 sts for every 4 rows on other long side of flap.

APPLIED I-CORD

With 2 strands of B, CO 3 sts on LH needle. Using dpn, *K2 sts, ssk (1 st from I-cord and 1 PU st from bag). Slip 3 sts back to left needle; rep from * until all sts have been worked. BO rem 3 sts. Sew BO edge to CO edge.

STRAP

With B, CO 155 sts.

Rows 1, 3, and 5: Purl with B.

Rows 2, 4, and 6: Knit with B.

Rows 7, 9, 11, and 13: Knit with A.

Rows 8, 10, 12, and 14: Purl with A.

Rows 15, 16, 18, and 20: Knit with B.

Rows 17 and 19: Purl with B.

BO all sts.

POCKET

Using A, CO 42 sts.

Work St st in following stripe sequence for a total of 15": A (3½"), B (2"), A (1"), B (2"), A (1"), B (2"), and A (3½").

BO all sts.

FINISHING

Strap

Allow the CO and BO edges to roll to WS. With WS facing you and 1 strand of B, sew each st from CO edge to each st of row 6, using overcast st (see page 92). This creates rolled edge on strap. Take care not to pull tightly. Sew BO edge to row 15 in same manner.

Felting

Felt both bag and pocket according to "Felting" instructions on page 93. Felt strap separately to avoid it wrapping around, and possibly felting to, the bag. To define shape of bag, place it over the box form to dry. After felting, strap can be cut to shorten length if desired and edges of pocket can be trimmed to eliminate rough edges.

Finishing Touches

Turn bag to WS. Using sewing needle and heavy-duty thread, sew strap to side gussets. Stitch pocket on back below flap. Turn bag to RS. Smooth surface with stiff brush. Trim excess fuzz and yarn tails. Sew on button.

Applied I-cord is worked around the top and the flap of the bag to outline the edge.

This is a vertical version
of the Messenger Bag.
Carry your books in this
hands-free, upscale satchel.
The slim look of this bag
is created by the vertical
shape and long shoulder
strap. It is great for students
and professionals alike.

SIZE (After Felting)

Finished Body Dimensions: Approx 12" wide x 14" tall x 4" deep

Finished Length: Approx 36" (shoulder to bottom of bag)

MATERIALS

Yarn: Cascade 220 from Cascade Yarns (100% Peruvian Highland wool; 100 g/3.5 oz; 220 yds) (4)

A: 7 skeins of color 8555

B: 2 skeins of color 8400

Needles: US 11 (8 mm) circular (32") and US 11 double-pointed, or size required to obtain gauge

Notions:

Removable stitch marker

Stitch marker

Heavy-duty thread to match A, and sewing needle

Tapestry needle

Box, 12" wide x 14" tall x 4" deep

Stiff brush or Slicker Brush (available at pet stores)

GAUGE

Gauge is given for knitting in the round before felting.

12 sts and 13 rows = 4" in St st with 2 strands of yarn held tog

STITCH PATTERNS

Stockinette Stitch (in the round)

Knit every rnd.

Stockinette Stitch (flat)

Row 1: Knit.

Row 2: Purl.

Rep rows 1 and 2.

Garter Stitch (flat)

Knit every row.

Note: Use 2 strands of yarn held tog throughout unless otherwise instructed.

BOTTOM

Using circular needle and A, CO 42 sts.

Work in garter st for 15 rows. Do not turn.

BODY

With 42 sts on needle, PU 14 sts along short side of bottom (gusset); PU 42 sts along CO edge; PU 14 sts on other short side (gusset)—112 sts.

PM, join into rnd.

Rnd 1: K42, sl 1 wyib, K12, sl 1 wyib, K42, sl 1 wyib, K12, sl 1 wyib.

Rnd 2: Knit.

Rep rnds 1 and 2 until piece measures 23" from PU rnd. End after working rnd 2.

K42, place removable marker in next st. BO next 70 sts with firm tension—42 sts.

FLAP

Working back and forth on 42 sts, knit 2 rows. Purl next row (RS).

Work in St st for 25". End after working a purl row. BO all sts with firm tension.

TRIM

Using circular needle and B, beg at removable marker, PU 14 sts across gusset, PU 42 sts across front, PU 14 sts across other gusset, PU 3 sts for every 4 rows on long side of flap, PU 42 sts across end of flap, and PU 3 sts for every 4 rows on other long side of flap.

Applied I-Cord

With 2 strands of B, CO 3 sts on LH needle. Using dpn, *K2, ssk (1 st from I-cord and 1 PU st from bag). Slip 3 sts back to left needle; rep from * until all sts have been worked. BO rem 3 sts. Sew BO edge to CO edge.

STRAP

Using circular needle and B, CO 155 sts.

Rows 1, 3, and 5: Purl with B.

Rows 2, 4, and 6: Knit with B.

Rows 7, 9, 11, and 13: Knit with A.

Rows 8, 10, 12, and 14: Purl with A.

Rows 15, 16, 18, and 20: Knit with B.

Rows 17 and 19: Purl with B.

BO all sts.

POCKET

Using circular needle and A, CO 42 sts.

Work St st in following stripe sequence for a total of 15": A (3½"), B (2"), A (1"), B (2"), A (1"), B (2"), and A (3½").

BO all sts.

FINISHING

Strap

Allow the CO and BO edges to roll to WS. With WS facing you and 1 strand of B, sew each st from CO edge to each st of row 6, using overcast st (see page 92). This creates rolled edge on strap. Take care not to pull tightly. Rep for BO edge, sewing to row 15.

Felting

Felt both purse and pocket according to "Felting" instructions on page 93. Felt strap separately to avoid it wrapping around and possibly felting to the bag during felting. To define shape of bag, place it over the box form to dry. After felting, strap can be cut to shorten length, and edges of pocket can be trimmed to eliminate the rough edges.

Finishing Touches

Turn bag to WS. Using sewing needle and heavy-duty thread, sew strap to side gussets. Stitch pocket on back below flap. Turn bag to RS. Smooth surface with stiff brush. Trim excess fuzz and yarn tails.

Contrast color is used for the I-cord trim
to define the outside edge and flap.

BOHEMIAN BERET

Good for a career outfit or a rendezvous in a city park, this beret makes a statement; it's contemporary and classic at the same time. The beret is knit in the round and felted.

Skill Level: Intermediate

◼◼◼◻

SIZE

To Fit Head Size: S/M (L/XL)

Finished Circumference: 22 (24)" after felting

MATERIALS

Yarn: 1 (2) skeins of Cascade 220 from Cascade Yarns (100% Peruvian Highland wool; 100 g/3.5 oz; 220 yds), color 8555 ❨4❩

Needles:

Sizes S/M: US 10 (6 mm) circular (24") and US 10 double-pointed, or size required to obtain gauge

Sizes L/XL: US 10½ (6.5 mm) circular (24") and US 10½ double-pointed, or size required to obtain gauge

Notions:

Stitch marker

Tapestry needle

Stiff brush or Slicker Brush (available at pet stores)

GAUGE

All gauges are given for knitting in the round before felting.

S/M: 14 sts and 18 rows = 4" in St st, using size 10 needles

L/XL: 12 sts and 16 rows = 4" in St st, using size 10½ needles

STITCH PATTERN

Stockinette Stitch (in the round)

Knit every rnd.

EDGE

Using size 10 (10½) circular needle, CO 78 sts. PM, join into rnd, taking care not to twist CO row.

Rnds 1–5: Purl.

Rnds 6 and 7: Knit.

Rnd 8: *K1, (K1f&b) twice; rep from * to end of rnd—130 sts.

BERET

Work in St st for 5 (6)" from inc rnd (rnd 8).

Work dec rnds as follows, changing to dpns when necessary.

Rnd 1: *K11, K2tog; rep from * to end of rnd—120 sts.

Rnds 2 and 3: Knit.

Rnd 4: *K10, ssk; rep from * to end of rnd—110 sts.

Rnds 5 and 6: Knit.

Rnd 7: *K9, K2tog; rep from * to end of rnd—100 sts.

Rnds 8 and 9: Knit.

Rnd 10: *K8, ssk; rep from * to end of rnd—90 sts.

Rnds 11 and 12: Knit.

Rnd 13: *K7, k2tog; rep from * to end of rnd—80 sts.

Rnds 14 and 15: Knit.

Rnd 16: *K6, ssk; rep from * to end of rnd—70 sts.

Rnds 17–27 (odd-numbered rows): Knit.

Rnd 18: *K5, K2tog; rep from * to end of rnd—60 sts.

Rnd 20: *K4, ssk; rep from * to end of rnd—50 sts.

Rnd 22: *K3, K2tog; rep from * to end of rnd—40 sts.

Rnd 24: *K2, ssk; rep from * to end of rnd—30 sts.

Rnd 26: *K1, K2tog; rep from * to end of rnd—20 sts.

Rnd 28: Ssk to end of rnd—10 sts.

Rnd 29: K2tog to end of rnd—5 sts.

Pull yarn through rem 5 sts. Fasten securely.

FINISHING

Allow edge to roll to WS of beret. Using tapestry needle, 1 strand of yarn, and overcast st (see page 92), sew rnd 1 to rnd 5 on inside of beret. Fasten off. Close all gaps. Work in all ends to WS. Felt according to "Machine Wash" instructions on page 93. Beret should measure 10½ (11½)" in diameter at the widest point, after felting. Allow to dry completely. When dry, use stiff brush to smooth surface of beret.

Optional top bead. Using size 10 (10½) needles, CO 5 sts. Knit 10 rows, cut yarn leaving 10" tail; you will have a 5 st x 10 row rectangle. Thread tail through tapestry needle; pull through 5 sts at top of rectangle. Weave along side of rectangle, across bottom 5 CO sts, and along rem side of rectangle. Pull tightly to draw up rectangle into a ball. Fasten off. Felt according to "Hand Wash" instructions on page 93 and sew bead to top of felted beret.

Strolling along on a cold winter day, you'll appreciate the charm and warmth of this fashionable scarf. The play of two colors allows it to coordinate with many outfits. This scarf features a double-sided stitch pattern, which makes it reversible, and a mélange of two colors, which makes it irresistible.

Skill Level: Intermediate

SIZE

Finished Measurements: Approx 6½" x 62" (excluding fringe)

MATERIALS

Yarn: Ultra Alpaca from Berroco (50% alpaca, 50% wool; 100 g/3.5 oz; 215 yds/198 m) 4

   A: 2 skeins of color 6245 Pitch Black

   B: 2 skeins of color 6207 Salt & Pepper

Needles: US 7 (4.5 mm), or size required to obtain gauge

Notions:
Size I-9 (5.5 mm) crochet hook

GAUGE

20 sts = 4" in patt; row gauge is not important for this scarf

SCARF

YO is not counted as a separate st in this patt.

With A, CO 32 sts.

Row 1: Sl 1 wyif, K1, *YO, sl 1 wyib, K1; rep from * to last 2 sts, sl 1 wyib, K1tbl.

Pick up yarn B from under yarn A.

Row 2: Sl 1 wyif, K1, *YO, sl 1 wyib, knit YO from previous row tog with next st; rep from * to last 2 sts, sl 1 wyib, K1tbl.

Row 3: Rep row 2.

Pick up yarn A from under yarn B.

Rows 4 and 5: Rep row 2.

Rep rows 2–5 until scarf measures 62". To make sure BO edge looks the same as CO edge, end with row 4 in color A.

Using A, BO as you work following patt: Sl 1 wyif, K1, *YO, sl 1 wyib, knit YO from previous row tog with next st; rep from * to last 2 sts, sl 1 wyib, K1tbl.

FRINGE

Cut 32 pieces each from A and B, 12" long. Using crochet hook and 1 strand of each color, attach fringe evenly spaced at each end of scarf.

FINISHING

Work in all ends. Block scarf, using method 1 on page 93. Trim fringe even.

The brioche stitch used in this easy, one-row repeat pattern is complemented by alternating colors and a nicely finished edge.

Golden Duet Tank 45

Tailored Skirt 47

ELEGANT AFTERNOON

Scalloped-Edge Purse 51

Watercolor Shawl 55

Tweed Polo 59

Triple-Pocket Bag 63

Driver's Cap 67

The classic tank has a contemporary twist achieved by the combination of two luxury yarns and the interchangeable necklines. It coordinates well with the Tailored Skirt and Watercolor Shawl or it can be worn with other wardrobe favorites. Any knitter will fall in love with this easy tank pattern.

Skill Level: Easy ●■□□

SIZE

To Fit Women's Size: XS (S, M, L, 1X, 2X)

Finished Bust: 35½ (38, 41, 46, 50, 55)"

Finished Length: 18½ (19½, 20½, 21, 22½, 23)"

MATERIALS

Yarn:

A: 2 (3, 3, 3, 4, 4) skeins of La Luz from Fiesta Yarns 100% mulberry silk; 210 yds; 2 oz), color 3324 ❸

B: 4 (4, 5, 5, 6, 7) balls of Glimmer from Karabella Yarns (90% rayon, 10% lurex; 50 g/1.75 oz; 141 yds), color 808 ❸

Needles: US 10½ (6.5 mm) straight, or size required to obtain gauge

Notions:

Size G-6 (4 mm) crochet hook

Tapestry needle

GAUGE

14 sts and 18 rows = 4" in St st with 1 strand each of A and B held tog

STITCH PATTERN

Stockinette Stitch

Row 1: Knit.

Row 2: Purl.
Repeat rows 1 and 2

Note: For back and front work in St st. When finished, purl side is used as right side of garment.

BACK

With 1 strand each of A and B held tog, CO 62 (66, 72, 80, 88, 96) sts. Work in St st until piece measures 11½ (12, 12½, 12½, 13, 13)" from CO edge. End after working purl row.

Armhole Shaping

BO 5 (5, 5, 6, 6, 7) sts at beg next 2 rows. Dec 1 st at each end every knit row 4 (5, 7, 8, 10, 11) times—44 (46, 48, 52, 56, 60) sts.

Cont to work in St st until piece measures 14½ (15, 16, 16, 17, 17)" from CO edge. End after working purl row.

Scoop Neck and Shoulder Shaping

Work both sides at the same time, K18 (19, 19, 21, 22, 24) sts, join second ball of yarn and BO 8, (8, 10, 10, 12, 12) sts, work rem sts.

Dec 1 st at neck edge every row 5 (5, 5, 4, 4, 5) times, then EOR 4 (4, 4, 5, 5, 6) times—9 (10, 10, 12, 13, 13) sts.

Work even until armhole measures 7 (7½, 8, 8½, 9½, 10)". BO all sts.

FRONT

Work same as back until piece measures 13½ (14, 14½, 15, 15½, 16)" from CO edge. End after working purl row.

Wide Neck and Shoulder Shaping

Work both sides at the same time.

K9 (10, 10, 12, 13, 13) sts, join second ball of yarn and BO 26 (26, 28, 28, 30, 34) sts, work rem sts. Work even until armhole measures same as back. BO all sts.

FINISHING

With reverse St st (purls) facing out, sew shoulder and side seams.

Armhole Picot Trim

With RS facing you, using crochet hook and 1 strand of A, join yarn with sl st at side seam.

Rnd 1: Work 64 (68, 72, 76, 84, 92) sc. Join with sl st to beg sc.

Rnd 2: Sc in first sc, *ch 4, sc in fourth ch from hook (picot), sc in next 2 sc; rep from * to last sc, make picot, sc in last sc, join with sl st to beg sc of rnd—32 (34, 36, 38, 42, 46) picots made. Fasten off.

Neck Picot Trim

With RS facing you, using crochet hook and 1 strand of A, join yarn with sl st at left front shoulder seam.

Rnd 1: Work 15 (17, 19, 21, 23, 25) sc along left neck edge, 26 (26, 28, 28, 30, 34) sc across neck, 15 (17, 19, 21, 23, 25) sc along right neck edge, 12 (14, 16, 18, 20, 22) along back neck edge, 8 (8, 10, 10, 12, 12) sc across neck, 12 (14, 16, 18, 20, 22) sc along left back neck edge—88 (96, 108, 116, 128, 140) sc. Join with sl st to beg sc.

Rnd 2: Sc in first sc, *ch 4, sc in fourth ch from hook (picot), sc in next 2 sc; rep from * to last sc, make picot, sc in last sc, join with sl st to beg sc of rnd—44 (48, 54, 58, 64, 70) picots made. Fasten off.

Bottom Picot Trim

With RS facing you, using crochet hook and 1 strand of A, join yarn with sl st at bottom left seam.

Rnd 1: Work 1 sc in every st around bottom edge, including 1 sc in center of each seam—122 (130, 142, 158, 174, 190) sc. Join with sl st to beg sc.

Rnd 2: Sc in first sc, *ch 4, sc in fourth ch from hook (picot), sc in next 2 sc; rep from * to last sc, make picot, sc in last sc, join with sl st to beg sc of rnd—61 (65, 71, 79, 87, 95) picots made. Fasten off.

Work in all ends. Block, using method 2 on page 93.

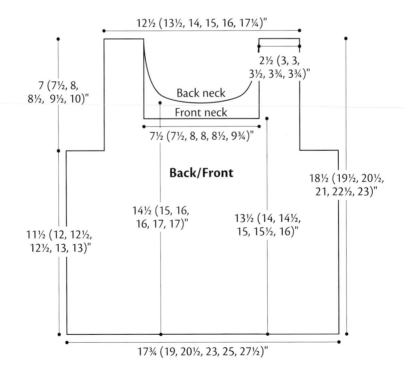

12½ (13½, 14, 15, 16, 17¼)"

2½ (3, 3, 3½, 3¾, 3¾)"

7 (7½, 8, 8½, 9½, 10)"

Back neck

Front neck

7½ (7½, 8, 8, 8½, 9¾)"

Back/Front

18½ (19½, 20½, 21, 22½, 23)"

14½ (15, 16, 16, 17, 17)"

13½ (14, 14½, 15, 15½, 16)"

11½ (12, 12½, 12½, 13, 13)"

17¾ (19, 20½, 23, 25, 27½)"

TAILORED SKIRT

Build your outfit for any afternoon around this silky and slimming skirt. Classic lines and rayon sheen make it suitable for many occasions. The silhouette is becoming for most figure types. Knit in the round, this is a great project for a novice knitter who wants to advance to the next level.

Skill Level: Intermediate

◖■■□

SIZE

This skirt is designed for a close fit.

To Fit Women's Size: XS (S, M, L, 1X, 2X, 3X)

Finished Hip (and Actual Hip) Measurement: 35½ (38, 40¾, 44½, 48, 51½, 55)"

Finished Waist (Excluding Elastic): 32 (34½, 36¾, 40, 43¼, 46¼, 49½)"

Finished Length: 27 (28, 28½, 29, 29½, 30, 30½)"

MATERIALS

Yarn: 10 (12, 14, 16, 17, 18, 19) skeins of Glacé by Berroco (100% rayon; 1.75 oz/50 g; 75 yds/69 m), color 2422

Needles: US 8 (5 mm), US 9 (5.5 mm), US 10 (6 mm), and US 10½ (6.5 mm) circular (24" to 29"), or sizes required to obtain gauge

Notions:

1 to 1¼ yds of 1"-wide non-rolling elastic for waistband

Stitch marker

Tapestry needle

GAUGE

All gauges are given for knitting in the round.

20 sts and 22 rows = 4" in 1 x 1 ribbing, using size 8 needles

18 sts and 24 rows = 4" in St st (main body), using size 9 needles

STITCH PATTERNS

Stockinette Stitch (in the round)

Knit every rnd.

Seed Stitch (in the round)

(Odd number of sts)

Rnd 1: *K1, P1; rep from* to last st, K1.

Rnd 2: *P1, K1; rep from* to last st, P1.

Rep rnds 1 and 2.

1 x 1 Ribbing (in the round)

(Even number of sts)

All rnds: *K1, P1; rep from * to end of rnd.

BORDER

Using size 10½ needle, CO 161 (173, 185, 201, 217, 233, 249) sts. PM, join into rnd, taking care not to twist CO row; marker indicates center back.

Work in seed st for 5 rnds.

SKIRT BODY

Dec rnd: K2tog, K14 (15, 16, 17, 18, 19, 20), [P1, K1, P1, K21 (23, 25, 28, 31, 34, 37)] twice, P1, K1, P1, K29 (31, 33, 35, 37, 39, 41), [P1, K1, P1, K21 (23, 25, 28, 31, 34, 37)] twice, P1, K1, P1, K14 (15, 16, 17, 18, 19, 20)—160 (172, 184, 200, 216, 232, 248) sts.

Rnd 1: K15 (16, 17, 18, 19, 20, 21), [K1, P1, K22 (24, 26, 29, 32, 35, 38)] twice, K1, P1, K30 (32, 34, 36, 38, 40, 42), [K1, P1, K22 (24, 26, 29, 32, 35, 38)] twice, K1, P1, K15 (16, 17, 18, 19, 20, 21).

Rnd 2: K15 (16, 17, 18, 19, 20, 21), [P1, K1, P1, K21 (23, 25, 28, 31, 34, 37)] twice, P1, K1, P1, K29 (31, 33, 35, 37, 39, 41), [P1, K1, P1, K21 (23, 25, 28, 31, 34, 37)] twice, P1, K1, P1, K14 (15, 16, 17, 18, 19, 20).

Rep rnds 1 and 2 for a total of 15 rnds.

Change to size 10 needle and work rnds 1 and 2 for 22 rnds.

Change to size 9 needle and work rnds 1 and 2 until skirt measures 24 (25, 25½, 26, 26½, 27, 27½)".

Change to size 8 needle and work rnds 1 and 2 for 10 rnds.

WAISTBAND

Work in 1 x 1 ribbing for 7 rnds.

Turning rnd: Purl.

Work in St st for 7 rnds.

BO all sts.

FINISHING

Work in all ends. Block skirt, using method 1 on page 93.

Cut elastic 1½" less than actual waist measurement. Fold waistband along turning rnd to inside of skirt and stitch bind-off edge to beg of 1 x 1 ribbing, leaving 1" opening. Insert elastic; sew ends tog securely. Stitch opening and block waistband again.

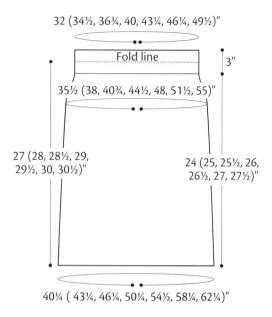

32 (34½, 36¾, 40, 43¼, 46¼, 49½)"

Fold line

3"

35½ (38, 40¾, 44½, 48, 51½, 55)"

27 (28, 28½, 29,
29½, 30, 30½)"

24 (25, 25½, 26,
26½, 27, 27½)"

40¼ (43¼, 46¼, 50¼, 54½, 58¼, 62¼)"

The seed stitch pattern on a background of stockinette stitch gives an illusion of panels to this tailored skirt.

SCALLOPED-EDGE PURSE

This beautiful lacy purse is a charming accent for the Elegant Afternoon outfit. Wear it over your shoulder or hide the chain inside to convert it to a handbag. Most of this purse is knit using a feather and fan pattern, and it is knit in the round.

Skill Level: Intermediate

SIZE

Finished Measurements: Approx 13" wide x 10½" deep (excluding handle)

MATERIALS

Yarn:

A: 2 skeins of Gelato from Fiesta Yarns (100% rayon ribbon; 4 oz; 262 yds), color 3127

B: 1 skein of Rayon Boucle from Fiesta Yarns (100% rayon; 4 oz; 240 yds), color 2127

Needles: US 7 (4.5 mm) straight and US 9 (5.5 mm) circular (20 to 24)", or sizes required to obtain gauge

Notions:

Stitch marker

Purse frame and 36" chain (See Lacis on page 95)

Tapestry needle

½ yd of fabric for lining

Thread to match lining

GAUGE

Swatch is worked in garter st flat. When gauge below is met, feather and fan patt will follow in its gauge. Use 1 strand each of A and B held tog until top band.

20 sts and 22 rows = 4" in garter st (flat), using size 9 needles

22 sts and 24 rows = 4" in feather and fan patt, working in rnd, using size 9 needles

STITCH PATTERNS

Feather and Fan Pattern (in the round)

(Multiple of 18 sts)

Rnd 1: *K2tog 3 times, (YO, K1) 6 times, K2tog 3 times; rep from * to end of rnd.

Rnd 2: Knit.

Rep rnds 1 and 2.

Garter Stitch (in the round)

Rnd 1: Knit.

Rnd 2: Purl.

Rep rnds 1 and 2.

Garter Stitch (flat)

Knit all rows.

PURSE BODY

To manage 2 yarns, place each ball into a small container and pull from center of balls.

Using size 9 needle and 1 strand each of A and B held tog, CO 144 sts. PM, join into rnd, taking care not to twist CO row.

Work in garter st (in the round) for 6 rnds.

Work in feather and fan patt until piece measures 9" from CO edge (measure from the deepest part of the scallop). End after working rnd 2.

On the next rnd, knit 9 sts. Cut yarn B. Place next 72 sts on holder.

TOP BAND

Change to size 7 needles.

Using A, work 72 sts on needle in garter st (flat) as follows:

(Odd-numbered rows are WS rows.)

Rows 1–3: Knit.

Row 4 (eyelet row): K1, YO, *K2tog, YO; rep from * to last st, K1—73 sts.

Rows 5–7: Knit.

BO all sts.

Place sts from holder onto size 7 needles. Work same as other side.

FINISHING

With RS facing you, lay purse flat. Pin out purse to meet schematic measurements. Match each top scallop with corresponding bottom scallop. Pin each scallop to define shape of scallops. Block, using method 2 on page 93.

Bottom Seam

Keeping corresponding scallops tog and with RS facing you, sew through both layers of scallops just above CO row with A. Work in all ends.

Lining

Cut 26¼" x 9¼" rectangle from lining fabric. With RS tog, fold the long side in half. Seam along side and bottom, about ¼" from outside edge. Place lining inside purse. Fold top of lining to WS and sew to first row of top band. Weave purse frame rod in and out of eyelets on each side. Attach chain.

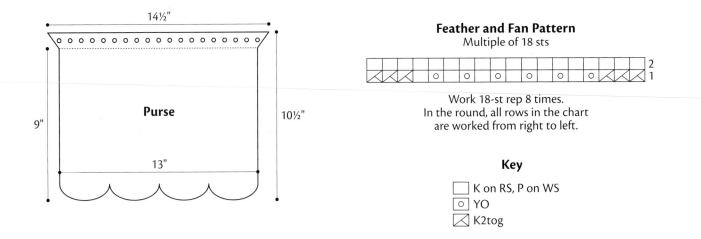

Feather and Fan Pattern
Multiple of 18 sts

Work 18-st rep 8 times.
In the round, all rows in the chart
are worked from right to left.

Key

K on RS, P on WS
YO
K2tog

A fabric lining adds background color and protection for your contents.

WATERCOLOR SHAWL

Whether you are wearing it as an accessory to your outfit, or to keep away the chill of a light breeze, you will look fabulous in this watercolor shawl. The interchange of stitch patterns as yarn texture goes from bouclé to smooth ribbon gives an effect of a watercolor painting.

Skill Level: Intermediate

SIZE

Finished Measurements:
Approx 54½" x 26" (excluding fringe) before blocking

Approx 61" x 28" (excluding fringe) after blocking

MATERIALS

Yarn:

A: 2 skeins of Gelato from Fiesta Yarns (100% rayon ribbon; 4 oz; 262 yds), color 3127

B: 1 skein of Rayon Bouclé from Fiesta Yarns (100% rayon; 4 oz; 240 yds), color 2127

Needles: US 11 (8 mm) circular (32"), or size required to obtain gauge

Notions:
Size J-10 (6 mm) crochet hook

GAUGE

11 sts = 4" in garter st using A, before blocking. Row gauge is not important for this shawl.

STITCH PATTERN

Lace Pattern
(Even number of sts)

Row 1: K2, *YO, K2tog; rep from * to last 2 sts, end K2.
Row 2: K2, *YO, P2tog; rep from * to last 2 sts, end K2.
Row 3: K1, *YO, K2tog; rep from * to last st, end K1.
Row 4: K1, *YO, P2tog; rep from * to last st, end K1.
Rep rows 1–4.

SHAWL

Note 1: To manage 2 yarns, place each ball into a small container and pull from center of balls.

Note 2: Alternate 2 rows A and 2 rows B as you work throughout entire piece. Loosely carry yarn not in use along side.

Using A, CO 4 sts.

Knit 1 row.

Work in patt as follows:

Rows 1, 3, and 5 (RS): K1f&b, knit to last st, K1f&b.
Rows 2, 4, and 6 (WS): Knit.
Rows 7 and 9: K1f&b, K1, *YO, K2tog; rep from * to last 2 sts, K1, K1f&b.
Rows 8 and 10: K3, *YO, P2tog; rep from * to last 3 sts, K3.

Work rows 1–10 a total of 14 times—144 sts.

Work rows 1–6 once more—150 sts.

Cont to use A, BO all sts loosely, leave last st on needle.

BORDER

Insert crochet hook into st left on needle. Work 77 sc along edge, 4 sc across bottom CO edge, and 77 sc along rem edge. Edge must be flat.

Fasten off. Work in all ends. Fringe is applied after blocking .

FINISHING

Blocking: Set steam iron to medium heat. Place it directly on shawl, steam and iron to flatten stitches. This treatment adds length and width to shawl as well as an exceptional drape.

Fringe: Cut 158 pieces, each 15" long, from A. Use crochet hook to attach 1 strand of fringe into each sc and tie additional overhand knot (see below). Work around outer edge of shawl. Trim fringe even.

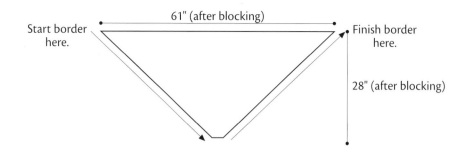

Start border here. 61" (after blocking) Finish border here.

28" (after blocking)

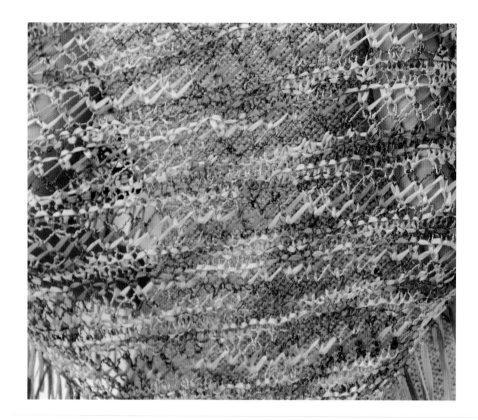

The combination of yarns and the open stitch pattern allow for the beautiful drape of the shawl.

TWEED POLO

This comfortable and elegant shirt has an interesting texture created by the oblong weave stitch pattern, which is flattering to the silky tweed yarn. Perfect for an elegant afternoon, this tried-and-true classic never goes out of style. Continuous flow of the stitch pattern at the seams gives an illusion of a garment knit in the round.

Skill Level: Intermediate

SIZE

To Fit Men's Size: XS (S, M, L, XL, XXL)

Finished Chest: 37 (40, 43, 46, 49, 52)"

Finished Length to Back Neck: 23½ (24½, 25½, 26½, 27½, 28½)"

Finished Sleeve Length to Underarm: 6 (6, 6½, 6½, 7, 7)"

MATERIALS

Yarn: 9 (10, 11, 12, 14, 15) skeins of Summer Tweed from Rowan Yarns (70% silk, 30% cotton; 50 g; 118 yds/108 m), color SH 507

Needles: US 6 (4 mm), US 7 (4.5 mm), and US 8 (5 mm) straight, and US 7 and US 8 circular (20"), or sizes required to obtain gauge

Notions:

4 stitch holders

2 removable stitch markers

Tapestry needle

Three buttons, ¾" diameter

GAUGE

16 sts and 25 rows = 4" in oblong weave patt, using size 8 needles

18 sts and 26 rows = 4" in 1 x 1 ribbing, using size 6 needles

17 sts and 25 rows = 4" in 1 x 1 ribbing, using size 7 needles

16 sts and 24 rows = 4" in 1 x 1 ribbing, using size 8 needles

STITCH PATTERNS

Oblong Weave

(Multiple of 6 sts + 4 sts. See chart on page 61.)

Rows 1, 3, 5, 7, and 9 (RS): *K4, P2; rep from * to last 4 sts, K4.

Row 2 and all even rows (WS): Purl.

Rows 11, 13, 15, 17, and 19: K1, *P2, K4; rep from * to last 3 sts, P2, K1.

Row 20: as row 2.

Rep rows 1–20.

1 x 1 Ribbing

(Even number of sts)

All rows: Sl 1 wyif, *K1, P1; rep from * to last st, K1tbl.

BACK

Using size 8 straight needles, CO 74 (80, 86, 92, 98, 104) sts.

Change to size 6 straight needles and work in 1 x 1 ribbing for 10 rows.

Change to size 8 straight needles.

For sizes XS (M, XL) only:

Work oblong weave patt as follows:

Rows 1, 3, 5, 7, and 9 (RS): Sl 1 wyif, K2, P2, *K4, P2; rep from * to last 3 sts, K2, K1tbl.

Row 2 and all even rows (WS): Sl 1 wyif, purl to last st, K1tbl.

Rows 11, 13, 15, 17, and 19: Sl 1 wyif, P1, K4, *P2, K4; rep from * to last 2 sts, P1, K1tbl.

Row 20: As row 2.

For sizes S, L, and XXL only:

Work oblong weave patt as follows:

Rows 1, 3, 5, 7, and 9 (RS): Sl 1 wyif, P1, K4, *P2, K4; rep from * to last 2 sts, P1, K1tbl.

Row 2 and all even rows (WS): Sl 1 wyif, purl to last st, K1tbl.

Rows 11, 13, 15, 17, and 19: Sl 1 wyif, K2, P2, *K4, P2; rep from * to last 3 sts, K2, K1tbl.

Row 20: As row 2.

For all sizes:

Rep rows 1–20 until piece measures 15 (15½, 16, 16½, 17, 17½)". End after working WS row.

Armhole Shaping

Work all dec sts in patt as est.

BO 5 (6, 7, 6, 7, 7) sts at beg of next 2 rows. Dec 1 st at each end EOR 4 (6, 6, 5, 6, 7) times—56 (56, 60, 70, 72, 76) sts. Work even until armhole measures 8½ (9, 9½, 10, 10½, 11)". End after working WS row.

Neck and Shoulder Shaping

Work 15 (15, 16, 19, 20, 21) sts and place on holder, BO 26 (26, 28, 32, 32, 34) sts for neck, work rem sts and place on holder.

FRONT

Work same as back until armhole measures 2¼ (2½, 2¾, 3, 3¼, 3¼)".

Placket Opening

Work 25 (25, 27, 32, 33, 35) sts, join second ball of yarn, BO 6 sts, work rem sts.

Cont to work both sides at once in patt until armhole measures 6¾ (7¼, 7¾, 8, 8¼ 8½)".

Neck and Shoulder Shaping

BO 5 (5, 5, 6, 6, 7) sts at each neck edge. Dec 1 st at each neck edge every row 5 (5, 6, 7, 7, 7) times. Work even in patt until armhole measures 8½ (9, 9½, 10, 10½, 11)". Place 15 (15, 16, 19, 20, 21) sts on holder for each shoulder.

SLEEVE (Make 2)

Using size 8 straight needles, CO 48 (48, 54, 54, 60, 60) sts.

Change to size 6 straight needles.

Work in 1 x 1 ribbing for 6 rows. Inc 2 sts on last row—50 (50, 56, 56, 62, 62) sts.

Change to size 8 straight needles. Work in following patt, AT THE SAME TIME inc 1 st in pattern as est at each end every 8 rows 2 (3, 3, 4, 2, 3) times.

Rows 1, 3, 5, 7, and 9 (RS): Sl 1 wyif, K2, P2, *K4, P2; rep from * to last 3 sts, K2, K1tbl.

Row 2 and all even rows (WS): Sl 1 wyif, purl to last st, K1tbl.

Rows 11, 13, 15, 17, and 19: Sl 1 wyif, P1, K4, *P2, K4; rep from * to last 2 sts, P1, K1tbl.

Row 20: As row 2.

Rep rows 1–20—54 (56, 62, 64, 66, 68) sts.

Work all inc sts in patt as est.

Work even in patt until sleeve measures 6 (6, 6½, 6½, 7, 7)" from CO edge.

Shape cap: BO 5 (6, 7, 6, 7, 7) sts at beg of next 2 rows. Dec 1 st at each end EOR 12 (12, 12, 13, 13, 13) times and every 4 rows 2 (2, 4, 4, 4, 4) times—16 (16, 16, 18, 18, 20) sts. BO all rem sts.

FINISHING

Block all pieces, using method 1 on page 93. Join shoulders, using 3-needle BO (see page 91).

Placket

Button band: Using size 7 straight needles, with RS facing you, CO 1 st. Beg at lower right edge of placket opening, PU 20 (22, 22, 22, 24, 26) sts evenly to neck edge—21 (23, 23, 23, 25, 27) sts.

Rows 1, 3, and 5 (WS): Sl 1 wyif, P1, *K1, P1; rep from * to last st, K1tbl.

Rows 2, 4, and 6: Sl 1 wyif, K1, *P1, K1; rep from * to last st, K1tbl. Place removable marker at end of row 4.

Row 7: As row 1.

BO all sts in ribbing.

Buttonhole band: Using size 7 straight needles, with RS facing you, beg at left neck edge. PU 20 (22, 22, 22, 24, 26) sts evenly along left side of placket opening. CO 1 st at end of row—21 (23, 23, 23, 25, 27) sts.

Rows 1, 3, and 5 (WS): Sl 1 wyif, P1, *K1, P1; rep from * to last st, K1tbl.

Row 2 (RS): Sl 1 wyif, K1, *P1, K1; rep from * to last st, K1tbl.

Row 4 (buttonhole row): Place removable marker into the first st, sl 1 wyif, K1, P1, K1, YO, K2tog, (P1, K1) 1 (2, 2, 2, 2, 3) time, P1 st 1 (0, 0, 0, 1, 0) time, YO, K2tog, (K1, P1) 1 (0, 0, 0, 2, 0) time, (P1, K1) 0 (2, 2, 2, 0, 3) times, K1 st 1 (0, 0, 0, 1, 0) time, YO, K2tog, (P1, K1) 2 times, K1tbl.

Row 6: As row 2.

Row 7: As row 1.

BO all sts.

Collar

Using size 7 circular needle, with RS facing you, beg at button band marker, PU 4 sts on placket, 12 (13, 13, 14, 16, 18) sts along right neck edge, 2 sts at right shoulder, 26 (26, 28, 32, 32, 34) sts at back neck, 3 sts at left shoulder, 12 (13, 13, 14, 16, 18) sts along left neck edge, and 4 sts on placket—63 (65, 67, 73, 77, 83) sts, ending at buttonhole band marker.

Row 1 (WS): Sl 1 wyif, K1, *P1, K1; rep from * to last st, K1tbl.

Row 2 (RS): Sl 1 wyif, P1, *K1, P1; rep from * to last st, K1tbl.

Rep rows 1 and 2 until collar measures 2".

Change to size 8 circular needle.

Cont in patt until collar measures 4¾". End after working row 2. BO all sts loosely in patt.

FINISHING

Sew buttonhole band to placket opening using mattress (vertical to horizontal stockinette st); see page 92. Place button band under buttonhole band. Line up bottom edges and sew them tog. Reinforce each corner of placket with extra stitching. Sew sleeves into armholes. Sew sleeve and side seams. Sew buttons to button band. Stretch edge of collar slightly as you block it. Work in all ends. Lightly steam seams.

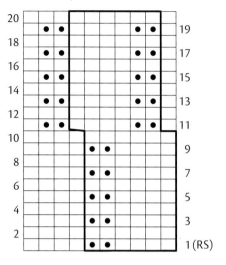

Oblong Weave
Multiple of 6 sts + 4 sts

Key

☐ K on RS, P on WS
⚫ P on RS, K on WS

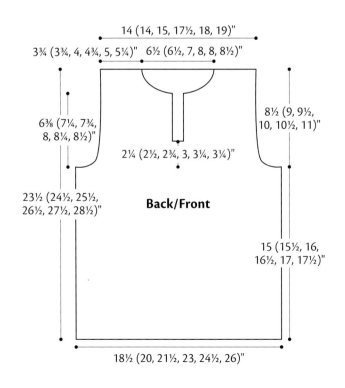

14 (14, 15, 17½, 18, 19)"

3¾ (3¾, 4, 4¾, 5, 5¼)"   6½ (6½, 7, 8, 8, 8½)"

6⅜ (7¼, 7¾, 8, 8¼, 8½)"

8½ (9, 9½, 10, 10½, 11)"

2¼ (2½, 2¾, 3, 3¼, 3¼)"

Back/Front

23½ (24½, 25½, 26½, 27½, 28½)"

15 (15½, 16, 16½, 17, 17½)"

18½ (20, 21½, 23, 24½, 26)"

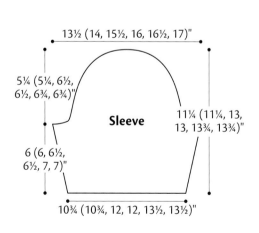

13½ (14, 15½, 16, 16½, 17)"

5¼ (5¼, 6½, 6½, 6¾, 6¾)"

Sleeve

11¼ (11¼, 13, 13, 13¾, 13¾)"

6 (6, 6½, 6½, 7, 7)"

10¾ (10¾, 12, 12, 13½, 13½)"

Use this fashionable and practical bag for hands-free convenience. The sturdy form, compact size, and three outside pockets bring about the bag's functionality. An unquestionably striking overall design includes details such as buckled straps for added security. The long strap becomes the side gussets as you sew the pieces together.

Skill Level: Intermediate

■■■□

SIZE

Finished Body Dimensions (After Lining): Approx 10½" wide x 11" tall x 2" deep

Finished Length: Approx 28" (shoulder to bottom of purse)

MATERIALS

Yarn:

A: 7 balls of Autunno from Di.Vé (100% fine merino wool; 50 g/1¾ oz; 98 yds/90 m), color 32991

B: 1 cone of 14/2 Euroflax Linen from Louet (100% wet spun long linen; ½ lb/225 g; 1300 yds), color 53 Caribou ❶

Needles: US 7 (4.5 mm) and US 8 (5 mm) straight, or sizes required to obtain gauge

Notions:

Tapestry needle

4 removable stitch markers

Size F-5 (3.75 mm) crochet hook

Two buckles, ¾" wide

Optional:

1 package InnerFuse Double-Sided Stiff Fusible Interfacing Heavy Weight by Dritz

1 yd of fabric for lining

Thread to match lining, and sewing needle

GAUGE

Use 1 strand each of A and B held tog.

23 sts and 44 rows = 4" in honeycomb st, using size 7 needles

24 sts and 36 rows = 4" in close st, using size 8 needles

25 sts and 35 rows = 4" in close st, using size 7 needles

STITCH PATTERNS

Close Stitch

(Multiple of 2 sts + 3 sts)

Row 1 (WS): Sl 1 wyif, knit to last st, K1tbl.

Row 2 (RS): Sl 1 wyif, K1, * sl 1 wyib, K1; rep from * to last st, K1tbl.

Rep rows 1 and 2.

Honeycomb Stitch

(Multiple of 2 sts + 3 sts)

Rows 1 and 3 (RS): Knit.

Row 2: K1, *Sl 1 wyib, K1; rep from *.

Row 4: K2, * Sl 1 wyib, K1; rep from * to last st, K 1.

Rep rows 1–4.

Note: Use 1 strand each of A and B held tog throughout unless otherwise instructed.

BODY

Using size 7 needles, CO 55 sts.

Work in honeycomb st for 10". Place removable markers at each end of row (points K and L on diagram on page 65) to mark front. Cont in patt for 2", place removable markers at each end of row (points M and N) to mark bottom. Cont in patt for 10" more for back. End after working RS row. Piece should measure 22" from CO edge.

FLAP

Change to size 8 needles.

Work in close st for 6". End after working WS row. BO all sts kw.

POCKET

Using size 7 needles, CO 59 sts.

Work in close stitch for 4½". End after working WS row. BO all sts kw.

SHOULDER STRAP

Using size 7 needles, CO 13 sts.

Work in close st until strap measures 61". End after working WS row. BO all sts kw.

BUCKLE STRAPS

Lower Strap (Make 2)

Using size 7 needles and 1 strand of A, CO 5 sts.

Row 1: Sl 1 wyif, K1, P1, K1, K1tbl.

Row 2: Sl 1 wyif, P1, K1, P1, K1tbl.

Rep rows 1 and 2 for 2". BO all sts in patt.

The two woven stitch patterns used in this bag are similar, yet different enough to draw attention to each design element. Although this bag is lined, it is not necessary to put in the lining if you want to make a soft, pouch-style bag.

Upper Strap (Make 2)

Work as for lower strap until strap measures 5½". End after working row 2.

Shape tip as follows:

Row 1: Ssk, P1, K2tog.

Row 2: Sl 1 kw, K2tog, psso.

Fasten off.

FINISHING

Work in all ends. Block all pieces using method 1 on page 93.

Trims

Using crochet hook and 1 strand of A, with RS facing you, work in following patt on BO edge of pocket, CO and BO edges of bag.

Row 1: Work 2 sc for every 3 sts across edge, end ch 1. Do not turn work.

Row 2: Working from left to right, sc in next st to right. Cont across row.

Fasten off.

Lining

Lay bag on top of interfacing. Using bag as a template, trace around edges. Place interfacing on top of two layers of fabric.

Cut through both pieces of fabric, adding ¼" for seams. Cut 2 rectangles of interfacing for gussets, matching dimensions of width of strap and height of front of bag. Cut 4 rectangles of fabric, matching dimensions of gusset and adding ¼" for seams. Fuse interfacing to fabric according to manufacturer's instructions. Place body of fused lining on top of knitted body and line up edges. Mark lining at points K, L, M, N. Sew 1 gusset to lining body from K to M, other gusset from L to N. Sew sides of left gusset to front and back of lining body. Rep for right gusset.

Assembly

Using 1 strand of A and tapestry needle, sew BO and CO edges of strap tog, using mattress (horizontal stockinette stitch) on page 92. This makes a flat seam. Center seam on bottom of bag. Sew each side of strap to bottom of bag.

With RS of bag facing up, place pocket RS up on top of bag body, with CO edge of pocket meeting edge of strap on bottom of purse. Sew pocket around 3 sides. Divide pocket into 3 sections by sewing through both layers of pocket and bag (to accommodate width of cell phone, address book, pen, etc).

Create gusset by sewing strap to left front and back of bag. Rep for right side of bag.

Insert lining, fold seam allowance to inside, and carefully stitch to bag using thread and sewing needle. When sewing lining to flap, fold flap slightly to create some ease as you sew lining to it.

Attach buckles to lower straps and sew to bag using 1 strand of A and tapestry needle. Attach upper straps to flap.

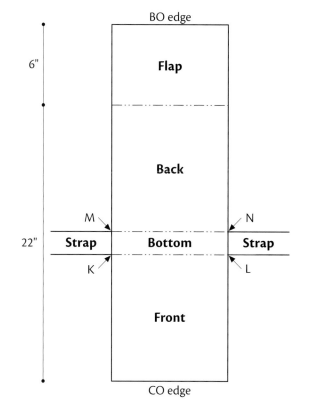

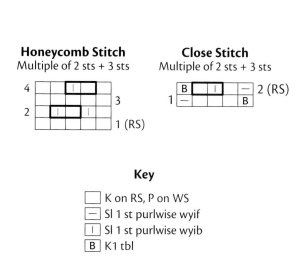

Key

- K on RS, P on WS
- Sl 1 st purlwise wyif
- Sl 1 st purlwise wyib
- K1 tbl

Inspired by a British driver's cap, this hat is richly textured. Do not let its distinguished appearance mislead you. It is suitable for everyday wear and has a unisex style. Although this cap has a unique structure, it is very doable. Detailed instructions navigate you through this project.

Skill Level: Experienced
◄■■▶

SIZE: One Size

Finished Circumference: To fit 22" to 24" head circumference

MATERIALS

Yarn:

A: 2 balls of Autunno from Di.Vé (100% fine merino wool; 50 g/1¾ oz; 98 yds/90 m), color 32991 (4)

B: 1 cone of 14/2 Euroflax Linen from Louet (100% wet spun long linen; 100 g/3½ oz; 570 yds), color 53 Caribou (1)

Needles: US 7 (4.5 mm) and US 8 (5 mm) circular (20 to 24"), or sizes required to obtain gauge

Notions:

2 stitch markers

1 stitch marker of different color

4 removable stitch markers

3 stitch holders

Tapestry needle

Plastic canvas, fine mesh

Head form

GAUGE

Use 1 strand each of A and B held tog throughout

23 sts and 36 rows = 4" in close stitch, using size 8 needles

16 sts and 23 rows = 4" in St st, using size 8 needles

16 sts and 28 rows = 4" in 1 x 1 ribbing (in the round), using size 7 needles

STITCH PATTERNS

Close Stitch

(Multiple of 2 sts + 3 sts)

Row 1 (WS): Sl 1 wyif, knit to last st, K1tbl.

Row 2: Sl 1 wyif, K1, *sl 1 wyib, K1; rep from * to last st, K1tbl.

Rep rows 1 and 2.

1 x 1 Ribbing (in the round)

(Even number of sts)

All rnds: *K1, P1; rep from * to end of rnd.

Stockinette Stitch

Row 1 (RS): Knit.

Row 2: Purl.

Rep rows 1 and 2.

TOP

Using size 8 needle and 1 strand each of A and B held tog, CO 19 sts.

Work in close st for 12 rows.

Inc Rows

Place removable markers at each end after row 16 (points K and N) and row 56 (points L and M). (See diagram on page 69.)

Rows 1 and all odd rows: Sl 1 wyif, knit to last st, K1tbl.

Rows 2, 14, 20, 26, 30, 46, and 52: Sl 1 wyif, K1f&b, *sl 1 wyib, K1; rep from * to last 3 sts, sl 1 wyib, K1f&b, K1tbl.

Rows 4, 6, 16, 22, 32–40 even, and 54–60 even: Sl 1 wyif, *sl 1 wyib, K1; rep from * to last 2 sts, sl 1 wyib, K1tbl.

Rows 10, 12, 44, and 50: Sl 1 wyif, K1, *sl 1 wyib, K1; rep from * to last st, K1tbl.

Rows 8, 18, 24, 28, 42, and 48: Sl 1 wyif, M1, *sl 1 wyib, K1; rep from * to last 2 sts, sl 1 wyib, M1, K1tbl.

Row 62: As row 4—45 sts.

Dec Rows

Row 1 and all odd rows: Sl 1 wyif, knit to last st, K1tbl.

Rows 2, 6, 12, 16, 22, 28, and 34: Sl 1 wyif, K2tog, *sl 1 wyib, K1; rep from * to last 4 sts, sl 1 wyib, K2togtbl, K1tbl.

Rows 4, 10, 14, 20, 26, 32, and 36: Sl 1 wyif, K2tog, K1, *sl 1 wyib, K1; rep from * to last 3 sts, K2togtbl, K1tbl.

Rows 8, 18, 24, and 30: Sl 1 wyif, K1, *sl 1 wyib, K1; rep from * to last st, K1tbl.

Row 38: Sl 1 wyif, *sl 1 wyib, K1; rep from * to last 2 sts, sl 1 wyib, K1tbl—17 sts.

BO rem 17 sts kw.

Before working side panel, block top, using method 1 on page 93.

SIDE PANEL

With RS facing you, PU sts around top in following order: beg at point K, PU 30 sts to point L, PU 61 sts to point M, PU 30 sts to point N—121 sts. See diagram on page 69.

Row 1 and all odd rows: Sl 1 wyif, knit to last st, K1tbl.

Rows 2–10 even: Sl 1 wyif, K1, *sl 1 wyib, K1; rep from * to last st, K1tbl.

Rows 12 and 16: Sl 1 wyif, K2tog, K1, *sl 1 wyib, K1; rep from * to last 3 sts, K2togtbl, K1tbl.

Rows 14 and 18: Sl 1 wyif, K2tog, *sl 1 wyib, K1; rep from * to last 4 sts, sl 1 wyib, K2togtbl, K1tbl.

Row 20: Sl 1wyif, K1, *sl 1 wyib, K1; rep from * to last st, K1tbl—113 sts.

Row 21: As row 1.

SHORT ROWS

See "Short Rows" on page 93. Refer to diagram on page 69.

Short Rows Right

Row 1: Sl 1 wyif, K2tog, (K1, sl 1 wyib) 17 times, wrap and turn.

Rows 2, 4, and 6: Knit to last st, K1tbl.

Row 3: Sl 1 wyif, K2tog, (sl 1 wyib, K1) 14 times, wrap and turn.

Row 5: Sl 1 wyif, K2tog, (K1, sl 1 wyib) 11 times, wrap and turn.

Row 7: Sl 1 wyif, *sl 1 wyib, K1; rep from * to last st, K1tbl (PU wraps as you come to them)—110 sts.

Short Rows Left

Row 8: Sl 1 wyif, K2tog, K34, wrap and turn.

Row 9: (Sl 1 wyib, K1) 17 times, sl 1 wyib, K1tbl.

Row 10: Sl 1 wyif, K2tog, K28, wrap and turn.

Row 11: K1, (sl 1 wyib, K1) 14 times, K1tbl.

Row 12: Sl 1 wyif, K2tog, K22, wrap and turn.

Row 13: (Sl 1 wyib, K1) 12 times, PU 17 sts at CO edge, PM (different color), join into rnd—124 sts.

BAND

Change to size 7 needle.

Work 1 x 1 ribbing as follows:

Rnd 1: K1, P1, *K1, P1, K2tog, P1, K1, P2tog; rep from * to last 2 sts, K1, P1, (PU wraps as you come to them)—94 sts.

Rnd 2: (K1, P1) 11 times, PM, (K1, P1) 18 times, PM, *K1, P1; rep from * to end of rnd.

Rnds 3–5: *K1, P1; rep from * to end of rnd.

Rnd 6: *K1, P1; rep from * to marker, K36 sts to next marker (36 visor sts). *K1, P1; rep from * to end of rnd. Place next 22 sts on holder, 36 visor sts on second holder, 36 rem sts on third holder.

VISOR

Using size 8 needle and with WS facing you, join yarn, beg working in St st on 36 top visor sts as follows, referring to diagram on page 69.

Row 1 (WS): P33 sts, wrap and turn.

Row 2: K30 sts, wrap and turn.

Row 3: P28 sts, wrap and turn.

Row 4: K26 sts, wrap and turn.

Row 5: P24 sts, wrap and turn.

Row 6: K22 sts, wrap and turn.

Row 7: P20 sts, wrap and turn.

Row 8: K18 sts, wrap and turn.

Row 9: P16 sts, wrap and turn.

Row 10: K14 sts, wrap and turn.

Row 11: P12 sts, wrap and turn.

Row 12: K10 sts, wrap and turn.

When working following rows, pick up all wraps as you come to them.

Row 13: P23 sts.

Row 14 (RS turning row): Purl to end of row.

Row 15: Working on bottom visor, sl 1 wyif, P22 sts, wrap and turn.

Row 16: K10 sts, wrap and turn.

Row 17: P12 sts, wrap and turn.

Row 18: K14 sts, wrap and turn.

Row 19: P16 sts, wrap and turn.

Row 20: K18 sts, wrap and turn.

Row 21: P20 sts, wrap and turn.

Row 22: K22 sts, wrap and turn.

Row 23: P24 sts, wrap and turn.

Row 24: K26 sts, wrap and turn.

Row 25: P28 sts, wrap and turn.

Row 26: K30 sts, wrap and turn.

Row 27: P33 sts.

Change to size 7 needle. BO 36 sts (PU wraps as you come to them). Do not fasten off. Place rem st on removable marker. Place 58 rib sts from first and third holders on needle. Fold visor along turning row. Place st from removable marker on left needle. K2tog, cont with ribbing patt until last st before visor, PU 1 st in corner of BO row of visor and put on left needle, P2tog. Work 1 more row of ribbing. BO all sts in patt.

FINISHING

Close opening by sewing top edges to side panel. Work in all ends. Block visor, using method 1 on page 93. Trace folded visor to plastic mesh and cut it out. Place it inside hat visor, sew to close. Block hat, using method 1 on page 93 to smooth and round corners. Dry completely on a head form. Allow top to come forward. Tack center of top to center of visor.

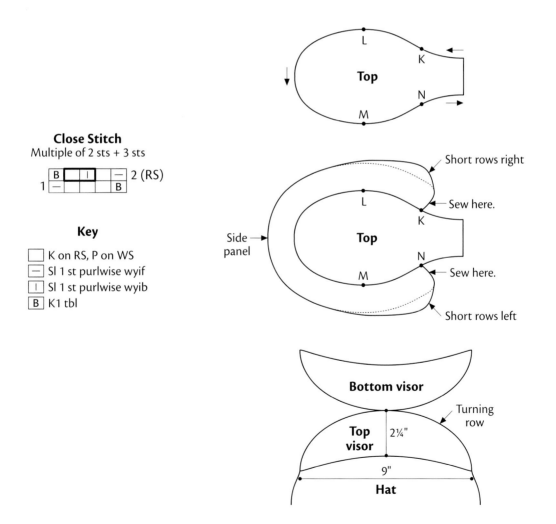

Close Stitch
Multiple of 2 sts + 3 sts

Key

- ☐ K on RS, P on WS
- − Sl 1 st purlwise wyif
- | Sl 1 st purlwise wyib
- B K1 tbl

Vintage Hat 73

Buttoned-Up Beanie 77

Lacy Scarf 79

GOTTA
HAVE IT

Gypsy Cable Scarf 81

Sheer Gauntlets 85

Fingerless Gloves 87

$\mathcal{V}$INTAGE $\mathcal{H}$AT

Influenced by the Art Deco period, this delightful hat can be worn in many different ways. When wrapped around the hat, the long attached tie plays a role in creating a turban or your own headdress. The textured edge, accomplished by the decorative cast-on, emphasizes the feminine and romantic look of this hat.

Skill Level: Intermediate

■■■□

SIZE: One Size

Finished Circumference: Approx 22⅛" (size is adjusted by wrapping tie)

MATERIALS

Yarn:

A: 2 skeins of La Boheme from Fiesta yarns (strand A 64% brushed kid mohair, 28% wool, 8% nylon; strand B 100% rayon boucle; 4 oz; 165 yds), color 11294

B: 1 ball of Kid Merino from Crystal Palace Yarns (28% kid mohair, 28% merino wool, 44% micro nylon; 25 g; 240 yds), color 204

Needles: US 10 (6 mm) circular (16" to 20") and US 10 double-pointed, or size required to obtain gauge, and US 15 (10 mm) straight for CO only

Notions:

Stitch marker

Tapestry needle

Head form

GAUGE

13 sts and 17 rows = 4" in 3 x 3 ribbing, using 1 strand each of A and B held tog and size 10 needles

STITCH PATTERNS

Seed Stitch

(Even number of sts)

Row 1: *K1, P1; rep from * to end of row.

Row 2: *P1, K1; rep from * to end of row.

Rep rows 1 and 2.

3 x 3 Ribbing

(Multiple of 6 sts)

All rows: *P3, K3; rep from * to end of row.

HAT

Using size 15 needle and 1 strand each of A and B held tog, CO 72 sts using decorative cast-on method on page 90.

Change to size 10 circular needle.

Work in seed st for 4 rows.

Work in 3 x 3 ribbing for 4 rows.

PM and join into rnd. Cont working in 3 x 3 ribbing until hat measures 5".

TIE-WRAPPING VARIATIONS

Rose. Bring the right tie around the forehead to the left ear. Bring the left tie to the left ear. Twist the ties together tightly. Hold the spot where the ties meet at the left ear with your left hand, and using your right hand, wind the twisted ties clockwise around that spot a few times, forming a rose. When done, tuck the tail ends into the center of the rose from behind.

Rope. Starting at the back, twist both ties together to form a rope. Bring the rope around the forehead to the back and tuck in the ends.

CROWN SHAPING

Work decs as follows, changing to dpns when necessary.

Rnd 1: *P1, P2tog, K3; rep from *to end of rnd—60 sts.

Rnd 2: *P2, K3; rep from * to end of rnd.

Rnd 3: *P2tog, K3; rep from * to end of rnd—48 sts.

Rnd 4: *P1, K3; rep from * to end of rnd.

Rnd 5: *P1, K1, K2tog; rep from * to end of rnd—36 sts.

Rnd 6: *P2tog, K1; rep from * to end of rnd—24 sts.

Rnd 7: *K1, P1; rep from * to end of rnd.

Rnd 8: *P1, K1; rep from * to end of rnd.

Rnd 9: *P2tog, K2tog; rep from * to end of rnd—12 sts.

Rnd 10: *K1, P1; rep from * to end of rnd.

Rnd 11: *P2tog; rep from * to end of rnd—6 sts.

Pull yarn through rem 6 sts. Fasten securely.

TIE

Using size 10 needle and 1 strand each of A and B held tog, CO 3 sts.

Turban. Bring each tie to the front, cross them over, and bring them to the back. Tie in a bow.

Border I

Row 1: K1f&b, K1, K1f&b—5 sts.

Rows 2, 4, and 6: Knit.

Row 3: Sl 1 wyif, K1f&b, K1, K1f&b, K1tbl—7 sts.

Row 5: Sl 1 wyif, K1f&b, K3, K1f&b, K1tbl—9 sts.

Body

Row 7: Sl 1 wyif, K7, K1tbl.

Row 8: Sl 1 wyif, K2, P3, K2, K1tbl.

Rep rows 7 and 8 until tie measures 73".

Border II

Row 1: Sl 1 wyif, K2tog, K3, K2tog, K1tbl—7 sts.

Rows 2 and 4: Knit.

Row 3: Sl 1 wyif, K2tog, K1, K2tog, K1tbl—5 sts.

Row 5: K2tog, K1, K2tog—3 sts.

BO all sts.

FINISHING

Work in ends. Block hat and tie, using method 1 on page 93. Place hat on head form to dry. After drying, fold tie in half RS tog. Fold hat RS tog. Place the folded edge of the tie in the opening at the bottom of the hat and sew through all 4 layers using 2 strands of Kid Merino held tog. This secures the tie and closes the seam. Block seam, using method 1 on page 93.

BUTTONED-UP BEANIE

Men and women alike gotta have this unique beanie, which brings style and function together. Turn down the brim to cover your ears on a windy or frosty day. The hat body is knit in the round, using a two-row pattern repeat. The unusual, but not difficult, construction of this beanie makes it fun to knit.

Skill Level: Intermediate

◼◼◼◻

SIZE: One Size to Fit Average Man or Woman

Finished Circumference: Stretches from 21" to 23"

MATERIALS

Yarn: 2 balls of Taos from Crystal Palace (100% wool; 50 g; 128 yds/118 m), color 4

Needles: US 10 (6 mm) straight, US 9 (5.5 mm) circular (16" to 20"), and US 9 double-pointed, or sizes required to obtain gauge

Notions:

Stitch marker

Tapestry needle

Two buttons, ⅝" diameter

Head form

GAUGE

17 sts and 36 rows = 4" in half-brioche st, using size 9 needles

STITCH PATTERNS

Half-Brioche Stitch (in the round)

(Even number of sts. YO is not counted as a separate st in this patt.)

Rnd 1: * P1, YO, sl 1 wyib; rep from * to end of rnd.

Rnd 2: *P1, knit YO from previous row tog with next st; rep from * to end of rnd.

Rep rows 1 and 2.

1 x 1 Ribbing (flat)

(Even number of sts)

All rows: Sl 1 wyif, *K1, P1; rep from * to last st, K1tbl.

1 x 1 Ribbing (in the round)

(Even number of st)

All rnds: *K1, P1; rep from * to end of rnd.

BRIM

Using size 10 needles, CO 58 sts.

Work in 1 x 1 ribbing (flat) for 7 rows.

Change to size 9 circular needle.

Cont in patt for 7 rows.

Next row: Sl 1 wyif, *K1, P1; rep from * to last st, K1, CO 32 sts using the single cast on (see page 78)—90 sts.

Join into rnd. From this point hat is worked in rnd.

Turning rnd: K58, PM for beg of rnd.

BODY

Work in 1 x 1 ribbing (in the round) for 6 rnds.

Work in half-brioche st (in the round) until hat measures 5½" from turning rnd. End after working rnd 2.

CROWN SHAPING

Work decs as follows, changing to dpns when necessary.

Rnd 1: *P1, K1; rep from * to end of rnd.

Rnd 2: *K2tog, (P1, K1) 4 times; rep from * to end of rnd—81 sts.

Rnd 3: *(K1, P1) 4 times, K1; rep from * to end of rnd.

Rnd 4: *P2tog, (K1, P1) 3 times, K1; rep from * to end of rnd—72 sts.

Rnd 5: *P1, K1; rep from * to end of rnd.

Rnd 6: *K2tog, (P1, K1) 3 times; rep from * to end of rnd—63 sts.

Rnd 7: *(K1, P1) 3 times, K1; rep from * to end of rnd.

Rnd 8: *P2tog, (K1, P1) 2 times, K1; rep from * to end of rnd—54 sts.

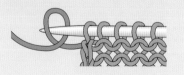

SINGLE CAST ON

Form a loop so that yarn from ball is in front of yarn coming from needle. Insert needle into this loop and tighten gently.

Rnd 9: *P1, K1; rep from * to end of rnd.

Rnd 10: *K2tog, (P1, K1) 2 times; rep from * to end of rnd—45 sts.

Rnd 11: *(K1, P1) 2 times, K1; rep from * to end of rnd.

Rnd 12: *P2tog, K1, P1, K1; rep from * to end of rnd—36 sts.

Rnd 13: *K2tog, P1, K1; rep from * to end of rnd—27 sts.

Rnd 14: *P2tog, K1; rep from * to end of rnd—18 sts.

Rnd 15: *P1, K1; rep from * to end of rnd.

Rnd 16: *K2tog; rep from * to end of rnd—9 sts.

Pull yarn through rem 9 sts. Fasten securely.

STRAP

Lay beanie flat with RS facing up. Fold brim up at turning rnd.

Using size 9 needle, PU 6 sts starting at point C (6 rows down from CO edge of side A of brim) going up to CO edge. See diagram below.

Row 1: Sl 1 wyif, (P1, K1) 2 times, K1tbl.

Rep row 1 for 8½".

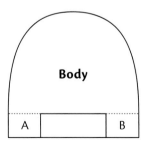

Body

A | B

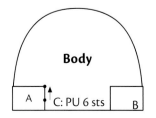

Body

A | C: PU 6 sts | B

Buttonhole and Tapered Tip

Row 1: Sl 1 wyif, P1, K1, YO, P1, K1, K1tbl—7 sts.

Row 2: Sl 1 wyif, P1, K2tog, P1, K1, K1tbl—6 sts.

Row 3: Sl 1 wyif, K2tog, P2tog, K1tbl—4 sts.

Row 4: Sl 1 wyif, K2tog, K1tbl—3 sts.

Row 5: Sl 1 wyif, K2tog—2 sts.

BO 2 sts.

FINISHING

Work in all ends. Block, using method 1 on page 93. Dry on a head form. Fold up brim. Sew 1 button at beg of strap, sew second button to beanie at the same level as buttonhole at end of strap.

LACY SCARF

If you want a scarf that's head turning, this is it! Have the pleasure of knitting it and enjoy the compliments. Luxurious yarn combined with an intriguing lace pattern makes this scarf exquisite.

SIZE

Finished Measurements:
Approx 6¾" x 74" (excluding fringe)

MATERIALS

Yarn: 2 skeins of La Boheme from Fiesta Yarns (strand A 64% brushed kid mohair, 28% wool, 8% nylon; strand B 100% rayon boucle; 4 oz; 165 yds), color 11294 [4]

Needles: US 10½ (6.5 mm), or size required to obtain gauge

Notions:
Size J-10 (6 mm) crochet hook

GAUGE

17 sts = 4" in patt. Row gauge is not important for this scarf.

SCARF

CO 29 sts.

Rows 1–4: Sl 1 wyif, K28.

Row 5: Sl 1 wyif, K1, *wrap yarn twice around needle, K1; rep from * to end of row.

Row 6: Sl 1 wyif, sl 3 sts wyib, drop all wraps. Put 4 tall sts back on left needle. Think of them as "1 st". Working in back of "1 st," K1, P1, K1, P1. *Sl 4 sts wyib, drop all wraps. Put 4 tall sts back on left needle. Working in back of "1 st," K1, P1, K1, P1; rep from * to last st, K1.

Rep rows 1–6 until scarf measures approx 73". Work rows 1–4 once more.

BO all sts.

FRINGE

Cut 52 pieces of yarn, 12" long. Using crochet hook and two strands of yarn, apply fringe evenly spaced at each end of scarf.

FINISHING

Work in all ends. Block scarf, using method 1 on page 93. Trim fringe even.

Detail of lace pattern

This scarf features an
uneven cable wandering
on a background of seed
stitch as it goes from color
to color.

SIZE

Finished Measurements:

6½" x 72" (excluding fringe)

MATERIALS

Yarn: 4 balls of Gypsy from N.Y. Yarns (90% acrylic, 10% wool; 50 g/1¾ oz; 88 yds/80 m), color 2 **⑤**

Needles: US 10 (6 mm), or size required to obtain gauge

Notions:

Size I-9 (5.5 mm) crochet hook

Cable needle

GAUGE

14 sts = 4" in patt; row gauge is not important for this scarf

BORDER

CO 30 sts. Work 4 rows in following patt: Sl 1 wyif, K28, K1tbl.

SCARF BODY

C6F (cable 6 front): Sl 3 sts to cn and hold at front, K3, K3 from cn.

Rows 1, 3, 5, 9, 11, 15, 17, and 21–33 odd rows: Sl 1 wyif, (P1, K1) twice, P2, (K1, P1) twice, K8, (P1, K1) twice, P2, (K1, P1) twice, K1tbl.

Row 2 and all even rows: Sl 1 wyif, P1, K1, P2, K2, P2, K1, P1, K1, P6, (K1, P1) twice, P1, K2, P2, K1, P1, K1tbl.

Rows 7, 13, and 19: Sl 1 wyif, (P1, K1) twice, P2, (K1, P1) twice, K1, C6F, K1, (P1, K1) twice, P2, (K1, P1) twice, K1tbl.

Row 34: As row 2.

Rep rows 7–34 until scarf measures 67". Work rows 7–25 once more.

BORDER

Work 4 rows in following patt: Sl 1 wyif, K28, K1tbl. BO all sts.

FRINGE

Cut 36 pieces of yarn, 12" long. Using crochet hook and 2 strands of yarn, attach fringe evenly spaced at each end of scarf.

FINISHING

Work in all ends. Block scarf, using method 1 on page 93. Trim fringe even.

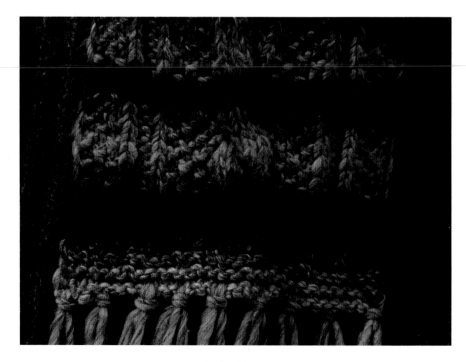

Detail of cable pattern

Gypsy Cable

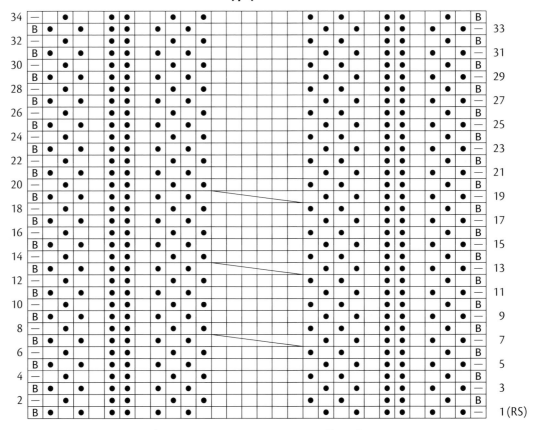

Work rows 1–6 once, rep rows 7–34 until scarf measures
approx 67". Then work rows 7–25 once more.

Key

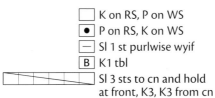

☐	K on RS, P on WS
●	P on RS, K on WS
—	Sl 1 st purlwise wyif
B	K1 tbl
▱	Sl 3 sts to cn and hold at front, K3, K3 from cn

SHEER GAUNTLETS

A companion to our Vintage Hat and Lacy Scarf, Sheer Gauntlets complete the romantic look of the set. Despite their delicate appearance, these gauntlets are surprisingly warm. A simple, lacy pattern with a two-row repeat makes it a quick knit and a great project if you want to learn to knit lace. Make a pair for yourself and another for a gift.

Skill Level: Easy ◖■☐☐

SIZE

Due to the elastic nature of lace patt, given sizes are sufficient for all adult women's sizes.

To Fit Women's Size: S/M (L/XL)

Elbow Circumference: 9 (10)" after blocking

Wrist Circumference: 7 (8)" after blocking

Length: 13 (13½)" after blocking

MATERIALS

Yarn: 1 ball of Kid Merino from Crystal Palace Yarns (28% kid mohair, 28% merino wool, 44% micro nylon; 25 g; 240 yds), color 204 ⬛**1**⬛

Needles: US 5 (3.75 mm), US 6 (4 mm), and US 7 (4.5 mm) straight, or sizes required to obtain gauge

Notions:
Tapestry needle

GAUGE

All gauges are given in lace patt before blocking.

21 sts and 22 rows = 4", using size 7 needles

23 sts and 24 rows = 4", using size 6 needles

26 sts and 26 rows = 4", using size 5 needles

STITCH PATTERN

Lace Pattern

(Multiple of 6 sts + 8 sts)

Row 1: K3 *YO, P3tog, YO, K3; rep from * to last 5 sts, YO, P3tog, YO, K2.

Row 2: K2 *YO, P3tog, YO, K3; rep from * to end of row.

Rep rows 1 and 2.

GAUNTLET (Make 2)

Using size 7 needles, CO 44 (50) sts.

Work in lace patt until piece measures 3½" from CO edge.

Change to size 6 needles. Cont in lace patt until piece measures 7½ (8)" from CO edge. This is the section where you can lengthen or shorten as desired.

Change to size 5 needles. Cont in lace patt until piece measures 9½" from CO edge.

Change to size 6 needles. Cont in lace patt until piece measures 12½ (13)" from CO edge. End after working row 2.

BO all sts kw.

FINISHING

Spray gauntlets with water. To open lace patt, pin out to measurements given on schematic. At CO edge, make sure to define scallops by pinning the points out at each P3tog. Let gauntlets dry. Sew 10 (10½)" seam beg at CO edge, skip 2" for thumb opening and sew rem 1". Work in ends.

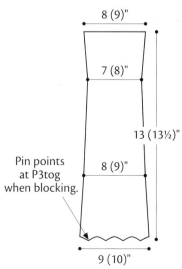

8 (9)"

7 (8)"

13 (13½)"

8 (9)"

Pin points at P3tog when blocking.

9 (10)"

Do you use your iPod, laptop, or BlackBerry on a cold day? Do you get in a car and your hands are freezing? You need to have fingerless gloves that keep your hands warm and fingers free. Knit in a simple rib pattern in the round using double-pointed needles, this is a fun and easy project for any knitter. If you've never used double-pointed needles, consider this project a great introduction to this useful technique.

Skill Level: Intermediate

SIZE

Due to the stretchy nature of rib stitch, given sizes will fit most adults.

Finished Wrist Circumference:
Approx 6¾ (8)" (not stretched)

Finished Length: Approx 7¾ (9½)"

MATERIALS

Yarn:

A: 2 balls of Taos from Crystal Palace (100% wool; 50 g; 128 yds/118 m), color 4 (4)

B: 1 ball of Aran from Crystal Palace (100% wool; 50 g; 102 yds/95 m), color 1019 (4)

Needles: US 9 (5.5 mm) double-pointed, or size required to obtain gauge

Notions:
Stitch marker

Tapestry needle

Size F-5 (3.75 mm) crochet hook

Small amount of waste yarn

GAUGE

26 sts and 24 rows = 4" in 1x1 ribbing (not stretched)

STITCH PATTERN

1 x 1 Ribbing (in the round)
(Even number of st)
All rnds: *K1, P1; rep from * to end of rnd.

GLOVE (Make 2)

Using B, CO 44 (52) sts. Divide sts evenly onto 4 needles. PM, join into rnd, taking care not to twist CO row. Work in 1 x 1 ribbing as follows:

Work 2 rnds with B.

Work 4 rnds with A.

Work 3 rnds with B.

Work 21 (30) rnds with A.

A total of 30 (39) rnds have been worked.

THUMB PLACEMENT

Right Thumb

Rnd 31 (40): *K1, P1; rep from * to last 9 (10) sts. Using waste yarn, knit next 6 (7) sts. (Leave 6" tails at beg and end.) This marks thumb placement. Return 6 (7) sts worked in waste yarn to left needle (waste yarn creates small row below). Using A, cont in patt over same 6 (7) sts and rem 3 sts.

Left Thumb

Rnd 31 (40): K1, P1, K1. Using waste yarn, knit next 6 (7) sts. (Leave 6" tails at beg and end.) This marks thumb placement. Go back to first st of 6 (7) sts worked in waste yarn. Using A, cont in patt over 6 (7) sts (waste yarn sts) and rem sts to end of rnd.

BOTH GLOVES

Cont in patt with A for 7 (9) more rnds.

Work 3 rnds B.

Work 4 rnds A.

Work 2 rnds B.

BO all sts in patt.

THUMB

Carefully pull out waste yarn. This creates gap with live sts. Put bottom 6 (7) sts on first needle, put top 5 (6) sts on second needle.

Right Thumb

Rnd 1: Join A and work first needle as follows: (K1, P1) 3 times, K0 (1), with third needle PU 4 (3) sts on left side of gap, (K1, P1) 2 (3) times, K1 (0) on sts from second needle, with fourth needle PU 3 (4) sts on right side of gap, PM, join into rnd—18 (20) sts.

Rnd 2: *K1, P1; rep from * to end of rnd.

Rep rnd 2 for 8 (10) more rnds.

BO all sts in patt.

Left Thumb

Rnd 1: Join A and work first needle as follows: (P1, K1) 3 times, P0 (1), with third needle PU 3 (4) sts on left side of gap, (K1, P1) 2 (3) times, K1 (0) on sts from second needle, with fourth needle PU 4 (3) sts on right side of gap, PM, join into rnd—18 (20) sts.

Rnd 2: *P1, K1; rep from * to end of rnd.

Rep rnd 2 for 8 (10) more rnds.

BO all sts in patt.

FINISHING

Work in all ends.

Lay right glove with the thumb facing down. Using B and crochet hook, chain 3 decorative stripes into knit sts (see instructions at right). Beg each stripe at top of ninth rnd above CO rnd.

For stripe 1, working into third (fourth) knit st to right of thumb, chain through only the top layer to approx 1" below BO edge. To separate fingers, cut yarn, leaving 12" tail. Bring tail through bottom layer.

Cont to chain through *both* layers to end. Fasten off. For stripes 2 and 3, skip 3 knit sts to right of previous stripe. Work same as stripe 1.

Work stripes on left glove as for right glove, reversing directions.

Block gloves, using method 1 on page 93.

CROCHETED CHAIN STITCH

Beg in knit row as indicated in Finishing. Using crochet hook, and yarn held on inside of glove, insert crochet hook into knit stitch and pull up a loop. *Insert hook into next st above, yarn over hook and pull through to front of glove, and through the loop on the hook. Rep from * for required length of stripe.

ABBREVIATION LIST

approx	approximately		P3tog	purl 3 stitches together—2 stitches decreased
beg	begin(ning)		patt(s)	pattern(s)
BO	bind off		PM	place marker
ch	chain		psso	pass slipped stitch over
CO	cast on		PU	pick up stitches by inserting right-hand needle into edge of fabric from right side and pulling a loop through it
cont	continue(ing)(s)			
cn	cable needle			
dec	decrease(ing)(s)		rem	remain(ing)
dpn(s)	double-pointed needle(s)		rep(s)	repeat(s)
est	established		RH	right hand
EOR	every other row		rnd(s)	round(s)
g	gram(s)		RS	right side
inc	increase(ing)(s)		sc	single crochet(s)
incL	increase left slant (see page 91)		sk	skip
incR	increase right slant (see page 91)		sl	slip
K	knit		sl 1	slip 1 st purlwise unless otherwise instructed
K1f&b	knit into front and back of same stitch—1 stitch increased		ssk	slip, slip, knit; slip 2 stitches knitwise one at a time to right-hand needle, insert left-hand needle from left to right into front loops and knit 2 stitches together—1 stitch decreased; left slant decrease
K2tog	knit 2 stitches together—1 stitch decreased; right slant decrease			
kw	knitwise			
LH	left hand			
M1	make 1 stitch; insert left needle from front to back under strand between last stitch knitted and first stitch on left needle, knit through the back of this loop		st(s)	stitch(es)
			St st	stockinette stitch
			tbl	through back loop(s)
			tog	together
			WS	wrong side
m	meter(s)		wyib	with yarn in back
oz	ounce(s)		wyif	with yarn in front
P	purl		yd(s)	yard(s)
P2tog	purl 2 stitches together—1 stitch decreased		YO(s)	yarn over(s)

The following techniques are used for the projects in this book.

LONG-TAIL CAST ON

For most of the garments, our preference for casting on is the long-tail cast on, unless stated otherwise. We believe that this method provides a nice edge and is elastic enough for most projects.

1. Make a slipknot, leaving a tail that is approximately three times the width of the piece that you want to make. Insert your needle into slipknot. Hold that needle with your right hand. Put your index finger on that stitch.

2. Bring left thumb and index finger through two strands (one from the ball, the other is the tail) from behind. Close other three fingers on left hand to hold both strands. Bring right hand down to form a V.

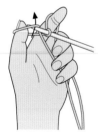

3. Insert the needle upwards under loop of the thumb, then over the strand of index loop. Bring the yarn through the loop of the thumb. Slip thumb out of the

loop and use it to adjust tension of new stitch.

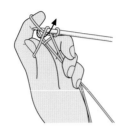

You have cast on one stitch. Rep step 3 until you have desired number of stitches cast on.

DECORATIVE CAST ON

This cast on is a variation of long-tail cast on (above). Please note that there are two yarn positions around the thumb that you need to alternate.

1. Estimate the length needed for long-tail cast on. Triple the length. Now fold this tail into thirds.

2. Position the yarn so that the thick part is over the thumb and the single strand coming from the ball is over the index finger. No slipknot is needed here. Insert the needle into the loop from the triple strand of the thumb, and under the single strand going over the index finger.

3. Using long-tail cast-on method cast on the first stitch.

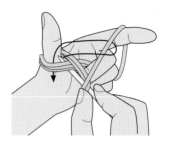

4. Slip the yarn off your thumb and rewrap it in the opposite direction, as shown below. Insert the needle under the three strands from the inside of the thumb, around the single strand of yarn from the ball, and then back under the same three strands to cast on another stitch.

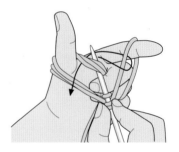

Alternate steps 3 and 4 (counting a stitch in each step as one stitch) until you have the desired number of stitches to cast on. There will be groups of two stitches on your needle. Make sure to work each stitch individually.

Separate each set of stitches when you start knitting.

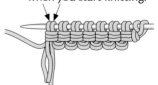

EDGE STITCHES

Most of our patterns are written to include edge stitches. At the beginning of each row, slip the first stitch purlwise with the yarn in front (sl 1 wyif). At the end of each row, knit the last stitch through the back loop (K1tbl). This technique makes nice edges.

THREE-NEEDLE BIND OFF

This bind-off method is used in place of shoulder seams. Both front and back shoulders should have the same number of stitches, which have been transferred from holders to needles.

1. Place shoulders right sides together. Insert a third needle into the first stitch of the first needle and the first stitch of the second needle as if to knit.

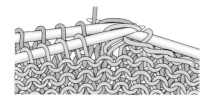

2. Knit these two stitches together and slip them off the needles. Repeat for the second stitch. Bind off.

3. Knit next stitch from each needle together, and bind off. Repeat until all stitches are bound off.

DECREASES

We use right-slanting and left-slanting decreases in our projects.

Right-Slant Decrease (K2tog)

Knit two stitches together—1 stitch is decreased.

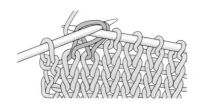

Left-Slant Decrease (ssk)

Slip 2 stitches knitwise one at a time to the right needle. Insert left needle from left to right into front loops and knit both stitches together through the back—1 stitch is decreased.

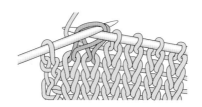

INCREASES

As with decreases, we use right-slanting and left-slanting increases in our projects.

Right-Slant Increase (incR)

Work the first stitch. Insert the tip of the right-hand needle into the stitch one row below next stitch on the left-hand needle. Lift that stitch onto the left needle. Knit the raised stitch—1 stitch increased.

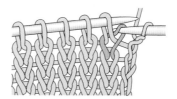

Left-Slant Increase (incL)

Work to the last stitch. Insert the tip of the left-hand needle into the stitch two rows below the last stitch. Lift that stitch onto the left needle. Knit the raised stitch through the back loop—1 stitch increased.

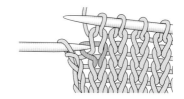

SEAMS

Several methods are used to create invisible seams. The overcast stitch is used for joining pieces to be felted.

Flat Stitch Seam

Place edges side by side. Insert needle under one half of a stitch on one side, and then one half of a stitch on the opposite side. Continue from side to side (like weaving), matching rows. To keep seam elastic, don't pull too tightly on the yarn.

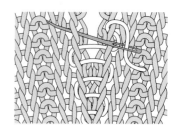

Mattress (Vertical Reverse Stockinette Stitch)

With the purl side facing up, place pieces to be joined together side by side. Insert the tapestry needle under one bar on one side, then insert the needle under one bar on the opposite side. Alternate sides picking up one bar at a time on each side. To keep the seam elastic, don't pull too tightly on the yarn.

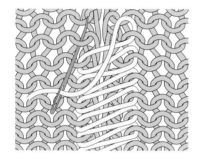

Mattress (Vertical Stockinette Stitch)

With right side facing up, place pieces to be joined together side by side. Insert the tapestry needle under one horizontal bar on one side, and then repeat on the opposite side. Continue working from side to side matching corresponding rows. To keep the seam elastic, don't pull too tightly on the yarn.

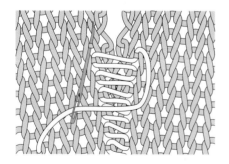

Mattress (Horizontal Stockinette Stitch)

This seam is used when joining two bound-off edges. The number of stitches should be the same for each piece. With right sides facing up, place bound-off edges together vertically, lining up the stitches. Insert a tapestry needle from back to front in the middle of the stitch of the lower piece. Go to the upper piece and insert the needle under the whole stitch. Repeat for the other side. The bound-off edges turn inwards and the seam is invisible. To keep the seam elastic, don't pull too tightly on the yarn.

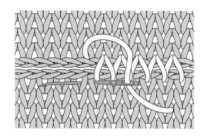

Mattress (Garter Stitch)

With right side facing up, place pieces to be joined together side by side. Insert the tapestry needle under one bar on the right side, return to the left side and insert the needle under one bar. Alternate sides, picking up one bar at a time. To keep the seam elastic, don't pull too tightly on the yarn.

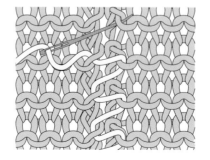

Mattress (Vertical to Horizontal Stockinette Stitch)

This seam can be used when you sew a sleeve to a sweater body. With right side facing up, place bound-off edge of one piece next to the side of the other piece. Insert the tapestry needle in the center of the stitch of the bound-off piece. Go to the upper piece and pick up one or two horizontal bars. Cont to alternate from one side to the other. To keep the seam elastic, don't pull too tightly on the yarn.

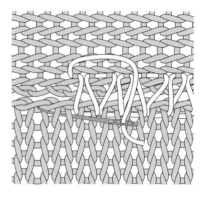

Overcast Stitch

With right sides facing up, place pieces to be joined side by side. Insert tapestry needle under one loop of the edge stitch on one side and go under one loop of the edge stitch on the other side. Continue to alternate sides. Draw the stitches close together, but not too tightly.

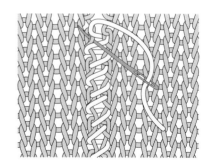

SHORT ROWS

This technique allows you to create shaping by working on only a portion of a row. Each row will stop at a certain point, and then you will wrap the next stitch and turn your knitting, depending on whether you're on a knit or purl row.

Knit-side short rows: With the yarn in back, slip the next stitch as if to purl. Move the yarn to the front of the work and slip the stitch back to the left needle.

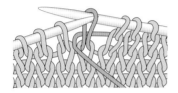

Move the yarn to the back of work. Turn the work.

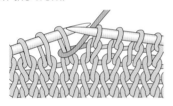

To pick up wrap on the knit side, knit to the wrapped stitch. With your right needle, pick up the front loop of the wrap knitwise, and knit the wrap and the stitch together.

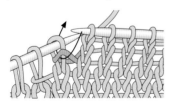

Purl-side short rows: With the yarn in front, slip the next stitch as if to purl. Move the yarn to the back of work and slip the stitch back to the left needle.

Move the yarn toward you. Turn the work.

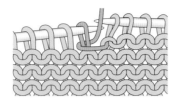

To pick up the wrap on the purl side, purl to the wrapped stitch. With your right needle, pick up the back loop of the wrap from back-to-front, and place it on the left needle. Purl it together with the wrapped stitch.

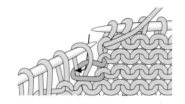

BLOCKING

You'll need the following tools to block your projects.

- Blocking board, towel-covered table, or any flat, waterproof surface
- Sturdy, waterproof pins
- Water spray bottle, good steam iron, or professional garment steamer

Blocking Method 1 (Steam)

A good steam iron or a professional steamer is used for this method.

- Lay piece (or pieces) flat. Pin to size. Hold steam source about 1/2" above surface, taking care not to touch the knitting with iron or steamer. Steam the desired area well. Remove steam. Let piece cool for a second. With your hands, shape and smooth seams as it cools. Repeat if necessary. Let piece dry completely.

- After garment is put together, steam it again, paying attention to seams. Lay flat to dry.

Blocking Method 2 (Spray)

Use a spray bottle for this method.

Pin piece (or pieces) to shape given in schematic or measurements given in finished measurements section of pattern. Spray with water. Dampen enough to relax the fibers. Allow to dry.

FELTING

Felting can be done by machine or by hand.

Machine Wash

Close all gaps created at any joins. Work in all ends on the wrong side. Put the finished item into the washing machine; use lowest water level, longest washing cycle, and hot water setting. Add 1/2 teaspoon of soap. Check the felting process every 10 minutes. Reposition the item during the felting process to prevent creases. You may need to use more than one cycle. To prevent permanent creases, do not let the item go through the spin cycle. Squeeze out excess water, and then roll the item in a towel to remove as much water as possible. Place over form if necessary and allow to dry completely.

Hand Wash

To felt top bead on beret, soak finished bead in hot water. Add a small amount of soap. Roll the bead in between the palms of your hands until it is firmly felted; this could take some time. Rinse it and let it dry.

STANDARD YARN-WEIGHT SYSTEM

Yarn-Weight Symbol and Category Names	Super Fine 1	Fine 2	Light 3	Medium 4	Bulky 5	Super Bulky 6
Types of Yarns in Category	Sock, Fingering, Baby	Sport, Baby	DK, Light Worsted	Worsted, Afghan, Aran	Chunky, Craft, Rug	Bulky, Roving
Knit Gauge Ranges in Stockinette Stitch to 4"	27 to 32 sts	23 to 26 sts	21 to 24 sts	16 to 20 sts	12 to 15 sts	6 to 11 sts
Recommended Needle in U.S. Size Range	1 to 3	3 to 5	5 to 7	7 to 9	9 to 11	11 and larger
Recommended Needle in Metric Size Range	2.25 to 3.25 mm	3.25 to 3.75 mm	3.75 to 4.5 mm	4.5 to 5.5 mm	5.5 to 8 mm	8 mm and larger

SKILL LEVELS

■□□□ **Beginner:** Project for first-time knitters using basic knit and purl stitches. Minimal shaping.

■■□□ **Easy:** Project using basic stitches, repetitive stitch patterns, and simple color changes. Simple shaping and finishing.

■■■□ **Intermediate:** Projects using a variety of stitches, such as basic cables and lace, simple intarsia, and techniques for double-pointed needles and knitting in the round. Mid-level shaping.

■■■■ **Experienced:** Project using advanced techniques and stitches, such as short rows, Fair Isle, intricate intarsia, cables, lace patterns, and numerous color changes.

METRIC CONVERSIONS

Yards x .91 = meters

Meters x 1.09 = yards

Grams x .035 = ounces

Ounces x 28.35 = grams

Contact the following companies to find shops that carry the yarns and other materials featured in this book.

Berroco
www.berroco.com
Glace, Ultra Alpaca

Bollicine
www.cascadeyarns.com
Dolly

Cascade Yarns
www.cascadeyarns.com
Cascade 220

Crystal Palace Yarns
www.straw.com
Kid Merino, Taos

Di.Vé
www.cascadeyarns.com
Autunno

Dritz
www.dritz.com
InnerFuse

Fiesta Yarns
www.fiestayarns.com
Gelato, La Boheme, La Luz, Rayon Boucle

Four Paws
www.fourpaws.com
Slicker Brush

Karabella Yarns
www.karabellayarns.com
Glimmer

Lacis
www.lacis.com
Purse frame and chain

Louet
www.louet.com
Euroflax 14/2

NY Yarns
www.nyyarns.com
Gypsy

Rowan Yarns
www.knitrowan.com
Cashsoft Aran, Summer Tweed

ABOUT THE AUTHORS

Faina Goberstein grew up in Russia, where, for many people, knitting socks was not a hobby. She made her first pair at the age of eight. Later she learned that there was much more to knitting than socks. While working as a design engineer in Russia, she completed a two-year course in knitting design. In 1980, she and her family immigrated to the U.S. Currently Faina works as a full-time instructor of mathematics at a community college and she continues to create and design knitwear, combining her technical background and knowledge of knitting. She lives in Chico, California.

Dawn Leeseman is a native Californian. She grew up in a very creative environment provided by her family. Although Dawn learned many crafts in her life, only knitting has remained her constant passion for the past 27 years. This love grew into a profession when she started working as an independent designer. Many of Dawn's original designs have appeared in national publications and have also been published by yarn and independent pattern design companies. She enjoys teaching, designing, and knitting in Chico, California.